Natalina's Kitchen

BRINGING HOMEMADE BACK

50 Recipes and Tips Inspired by Italian Mammas

ITALIANCOOKINGSCHOOLGUELPH.COM

f *natalinaskitchen*   🐦 *@natalinaskitch*   📷 *@natalinaskitchen*

TABLE OF CONTENTS

THIS IS DEDICATED TO ITALIAN WOMEN OF
DAYS GONE PAST: THE WOMEN WHO TIRELESSLY
COOKED FOR THEIR FAMILY AND FRIENDS, WHO
OFTEN MISSED OUT ON THE FUN, BECAUSE THEY
WERE AT HOME IN THE KITCHEN. THE MAMMAS,
THE ZIAS, BUT MOST OF ALL, THE NONNAS!

Nonna. What exactly does it mean? *Nonna* is the Italian word for Grandmother. A typical Nonna, in my opinion, is a warm, loving woman that spends loads of time in the family kitchen and wants nothing more than to feed everyone! The daily meals and the meals for special occasions are carefully planned events, and if there's a Nonna involved, she usually takes the lead role in the production.

I have fond childhood memories of my mother, her three sisters, and my Nonna all cooking together for family get-togethers. Everything was approved by Nonna: the menu, the quantities, the ingredients used, and ultimately, the final tasting. It was a joy to watch the five of them cooking together. There was such respect for my Nonna, from addressing her in the formal Italian to letting her have the final say.

Natalizia Marchesano was a strong woman that lived until she was 95, and I miss her. Along with two of my cousins, I am named after her, and my only daughter's middle name commemorates her. She wanted nothing more in her life than to take care of her family. These were simpler times and she was a career housewife. Everything was made from scratch. *Everything!* Most of the produce was grown in the garden and it was either canned or frozen for the winter. I think Nonna would be proud of me and my cooking school. I often feel her presence in my school.

My mother learned to cook from my Nonna while still living in southern Italy. My mother was 19 years old when she married my father and immigrated to Canada, and my mother is the best cook I know. Her Italian dishes were lovingly prepared with homegrown produce and the best quality ingredients. They didn't vacation regularly, but their six children (and whoever else was sitting around the table) always had the best to eat. There was a sense of pride around serving everyone the food of their ancestral hometown.

I think the thing that most impressed me about my mom's cooking were the dishes she made that *weren't* Italian. English was her second language and she quickly adapted to a Canadian lifestyle. She wanted to learn the dishes of her adopted country and prepare them well for her family. This included apple pie, roast beef, pancakes, and a Thanksgiving dinner with all the trimmings. Of course, these dishes were sometimes infused with a little bit of Italy, but always lovingly prepared to perfection. The first cookbook I owned was a book I grew up with in my Mom's kitchen: *The Good Housekeeping Illustrated Cookbook*.

I started cooking when I was about 11 years old. Since my mother was such a good cook, I started baking first. With a busy family, my mother didn't always have time to bake, and Sundays became my day to bake dessert for family dinner. I always challenged myself with new, advanced recipes, and I tested them out on my four brothers. It was the perfect learning environment. I baked, and they loved to eat, so I quickly gained confidence. When I was engaged to be married, my mother told me that I would need to help make Sunday dinner with her from now on so she could teach me to cook. I had helped her for about three weeks when she quickly realized that I had paid a lot more attention than she realized. She dismissed me from the Sunday ritual.

My own daughter Laura, currently 14 years old, also started cooking at age 11. She started with the same pancake recipe I did, from the same cookbook. She loves to bake and I encourage her to cook whenever the urge hits. There are things she is learning in my kitchen by default, and others I teach her and my three sons.

My two oldest sons, Alex and Michael, both enjoy cooking for entirely different reasons. One enjoys experimenting in the kitchen, while the other just cooks because he loves good food!

My third son, Stefano, seems to not have an interest at all. I am hoping this will change, or he may have to sing for his supper. He may get that from his father – the non-interest in cooking, not the singing! My husband, Bob, and I have a great thing going: he grows beautiful produce in the garden, and I cook it. It seems to work!

This cookbook is the story of homemade food in my family. The recipes have been passed down from one generation to the next. After living in Italy for a few years, I gained an even deeper understanding of the Italian food culture and the importance of family recipes. When we returned to Canada, it was then that I realized what a gift my mother had given me. Not all families have kept these family traditions alive, and I wanted to preserve this for my own family, and to share with you.

My cooking school was born out of this, and the recipes in this cookbook are the same ones that I began teaching in my school. Some are my interpretation of the Southern Italian or Calabrese dishes I grew up with. Some are favourites I enjoyed while living in Milan, in northern Italy. Some are just classic Italian dishes. For the most part, they are authentic Italian recipes, or they have evolved from classic Italian flavours.

This book and my school would not be possible without the Nonnas, including my own late Nonnas, and my mother, Palma Bombino, who is the quintessential Nonna. I thank them for cooking tirelessly for their families and sharing their knowledge, recipes and techniques with the next generations. It sounds simple, but it is so important. In some families these traditions have been lost.

After all, it's not just about the food and nourishing our bodies, but taking the time to lovingly prepare a meal and sit down with family at least once a day to spend time together. This is one of the most important rituals that we as humans can experience on a daily basis: breaking bread together. Thank you, Mom, for instilling this in me.

NATALINA'S PANTRY AND TIPS

On any given day, I have each of the following ingredients in my pantry. Having these on hand at all times ensures that I can put together an authentic Italian meal at a moment's notice!

Virgin olive oil from my parents' hometown in Calabria, Italy. This is what I cook with. There are not many virgin olive oils on the market, so you may have to substitute an inferior extra virgin olive oil or a blend. Very few extra virgin olive oils on the market are actually extra virgin olive oil. Using authentic, Italian olive oil in your Italian dishes will elevate their quality instantly! Learn more about how to choose olive oil on page 93.

Extra Virgin Olive Oil from my parent's home town in Calabria, Italy. This is what I finish with, and I use it raw to get all the wonderful health benefits. A true extra virgin has 0.8% acidity or lower, and this is one of the fundamentals of the Mediterranean diet. A generous drizzle on most dishes to finish will immediately take your dishes a step closer to an authentic Italian dish.

Grape seed oil. I love using olive oil in my dishes for the flavour and health benefits, but it doesn't have a high smoke point for frying. Instead, I use grape seed oil as a great flavourless oil for frying.

High-quality canned tomatoes: Whether they are pureed (*passata*) or plum, the tomatoes I use are of the finest quality, with as few ingredients as possible (tomatoes and salt, maybe basil). Whether home-canned or commercial, San Marzano (DOP) or Roma from Italy, they all have a place in my kitchen depending on the application. If tomatoes are the star of the dish, then the tomatoes should be top quality! Find my tips for choosing canned tomatoes on page 61.

Sea salt and regular table salt: Coarse or fine, depending on the dish. Seasoning a dish properly is very important, and finishing something that comes out of the fryer with coarse sea salt just adds a nice finish.

Pepper: Ground black pepper and freshly-ground black pepper are used to season dishes or bring out the best in the ingredients. I often use crushed chillies in my kitchen to add heat, and my ancestral region of Calabria is known for its chillies. For use in my kitchen, we grow our own or buy imported from Calabria.

Balsamic vinegar from Modena (DOP): An authentic balsamic from Modena only has 2 ingredients: cooked grape must and wine vinegar. I use this regularly in salad, so I usually have a standard one for daily use and an aged one for special dishes. You can reduce it yourself to create a glaze (*see page 11*).

Parmesan cheese: Having lived in Milan for a number of years, I am undoubtedly addicted to Parmigiano Reggiano (DOP), but 100% Canadian parmesan with no fillers also finds a place in my kitchen. Typically I will use domestic parmesan in large quantities (such as in a filling), and finish with the Cadillac of cheeses: Parmigiano Reggiano!

Fresh basil is used very generously in my kitchen, and I never use dried. If I have an abundance of it left over in my garden at the end of the season, I wash and air dry it, and then chop it in the food processor with a little olive oil to form a paste. I will then freeze this in freezer bags and break off a piece as needed to add to sauces. Fresh is best, but frozen is better than dried. Fresh herbs will always elevate your cooking.

Other fresh herbs: My garden is usually full of fresh herbs from the spring to winter, and I use them generously. Fresh herbs can make a huge difference in your results and enhance your dishes. The only dried herb I typically use is Italian oregano. We dry our own, or I recommend Italian oregano from Calabria or Sicily, often sold still on the stem.

Garlic: Contrary to popular belief, not all Italians use a lot of garlic in their cooking. Italian cuisine is very regional, and some regions use it more than others. In the region of Calabria, where my family is from, we use garlic *or* onions in tomato sauce, but never both. We typically flavour the oil with a crushed clove and then remove it. This action provides a slight garlic flavour that is not overpowering. I always use fresh garlic from my garden and store it in the cantina all winter.

Dried bread/crumbs: Leftover bread is placed in a cool oven to dry out. Your oven should be airtight to keep the bread from getting stale or moldy. When I have accumulated some, I place this bread in the food processor to finely grate. Bags of bread crumbs in the freezer will stay fresh for some time.

Flour: I always have several flour varieties on hand, including Canadian all-purpose; 00 imported from Italy; semola from Italy; hard wheat flour; whole wheat flour; and pastry flour. Specialty flours always guarantee a better result, depending on the recipe. Authentic Italian recipes call for Italian-style flours as they are milled differently (usually more finely) than domestic flours. See pages 21 and 29 for more on the differences between Canadian and Italian flours.

Dry pasta: I always have dry pasta in my pantry, and the shapes vary. Some are long such as spaghetti or linguine; others are short such as penne or rigatoni. I prefer pasta imported from Italy, as it tends to be higher quality than Canadian pasta.

Wine and spirits: Wine can add a lot of flavour to a dish, or can simply be used to deglaze the pan. If I am making a light-coloured dish or a more delicate dish, I will use a dry white, such as a pinot grigio. If I am cooking red meat or something more robust, I use a dry red wine. I like something from the south of Italy, such as a primitivo. I always have dry and sweet Marsala in my cupboard. This fortified wine used in both sweet and savoury dishes is a must in my kitchen.

Charcuterie: We make our own cacciatore salami, soppressata salami and capacollo. We shrink-wrap it and refrigerate it so we have it all year long. I also like to add some authentic prosciutto di Parma (DOP) to an antipasto platter.

Antipasti
Appetizers

HOW TO BUY BALSAMIC VINEGAR

I love balsamic vinegar! I came to really appreciate it when we lived in Italy. I also developed a palate for some very good ones.

My students often ask me what to look for when buying one, and there really are only a few things to consider:

- Balsamic vinegar from Modena DOP is the best. They developed the age old tradition of producing it and no one does it better.

- It should have the "DOP" symbol on it. Like other protected culinary products, your balsamic vinegar should be monitored to comply with the traditional methods and recipes.

- It should *only* have two ingredients listed: cooked grape must and wine vinegar. There should not be caramel or colour listed.

- The older it is, the sweeter, more intense, and usually more expensive it is. Different ages have a place in different recipes. For example, I would use a younger balsamic in a marinade and an older one served with fresh strawberries.

There are many new balsamic products popping up such as glazes and cremes. They can be expensive, and many don't use authentic balsamic from Modena, so be careful when making your purchase. You can make your own glaze by just reducing balsamic vinegar yourself (*see instructions below*).

HOW TO STORE BASIL AND PARSLEY FOR THE LONG TERM

How many times have you bought a bunch of basil or parsley for a recipe and had the majority rot before you could use it all?

When these herbs are in season, it's a great time to get them from the farmers' market (or your own garden) and store it for use later.

Here's how to make them last.

1. Wash the fresh basil (or parsley) under cool running water or fill the sink and soak. Remove all the sand & dirt and shake off excess water.

2. Spread all the clean herbs on a clean tea towel and let it air dry.

3. Remove all the course stems and bruised, discoloured or tough leaves.

4. Add the leaves and tender stems to a food processor and pulse until you have it chopped finely. Add enough olive oil or canola oil to create a paste. A large bowl of your food processor packed loosely might need about 3 tablespoons of oil.

5. Using a spatula, scrape it into a freezer bag with a zip closure. Remove all the air before closing the bag.

Store in the freezer and break off a piece each time you need some fresh basil/parsley. I throw it frozen right into sauces and it is the next best thing to fresh – without any waste!

BALSAMIC GLAZE

1 cup of Balsamic from Modena, DOP, not aged

Pour the balsamic vinegar into a non-stick frying pan and place over high heat. Bring to a boil and then down to simmer. Simmer until desired consistency is reached. Pour into a bowl to cool, and then a squirt bottle. Great for a garnish on a salad or dessert that is so delicious.... or a pizza to add a bit of sweet and salty!

BASIL PESTO & GOAT'S CHEESE CROSTINI

I love basil pesto and have it on hand all the time. I invented this as a quick antipasto when some unexpected guests dropped by and we wanted a small bite to have with wine. The complex flavours of the basil pesto pair nicely with the mild goat's cheese. Another mild, spreadable cheese could also be used.

½ batch of Basil Pesto (see recipe on page 45)

1 baguette

⅓ cup olive oil for brushing

1 large clove of garlic

2 cups of goat's cheese, approximately

Preheat the oven to 400°F. Slice the baguette into slices on the diagonal, and place the bread slices on a cookie sheet.

Brush the top of each slice lightly with olive oil. Toast in the pre-heated oven for approximately 8 minutes or until golden.

Remove from the oven and rub the peeled garlic clove on each piece.

Spread a generous amount of goat's cheese on each crostini and add a dollop of basil pesto on top.

Yield: 6 Persons

BRUSCHETTA

Bruschetta is simply a crostini with a seasonal topping. It could be mushrooms, pate or a number of other things. Tomatoes are the most common and this is my version.

1 French bread stick, sliced diagonally into slices

3-4 seasonal, fresh tomatoes, cut into small cubes

1 large or 2 small garlic cloves, minced + 1 large for rubbing on the bread

4 long green onions, sliced into rounds

½ teaspoon of Italian dried oregano

Salt to taste

¼ cup of extra virgin olive oil; extra for brushing bread

¼ cup Italian parmesan cheese, grated

Preheat the oven to 400°F. Place bread slices on a cookie sheet, brush lightly with olive oil and toast in the oven approximately 8 minutes.

Meanwhile, place the tomatoes, garlic and green onions in a medium bowl. Stir and season well with salt. Taste and adjust seasoning until the tomato flavour shines. Add oregano and olive oil; stir. Taste and adjust seasonings and olive oil.

Remove toasted bread slices from the oven and rub the peeled garlic clove on each piece. Top each slice with tomato topping and a sprinkle of parmesan cheese. Serve!

Yield: 4-6 Persons

FUNGHI FRITTI

FRIED MUSHROOMS WITH VINCOTTO

I love mushrooms and I have fond memories of picking them in the vacant lot at the end of my Nonna's street. We would find them and then seek Nonna's approval as to whether they were "good" or not. And by "good", I mean not poison! Nonna could tell just by looking at them. When they were boiled it was an old wives tail to add garlic and a gold wedding band. I think the story goes that if they turn black they were poison. Of course, I would never pick wild mushrooms now as it is far too risky and Nonna is no longer with us to make sure!

This recipe is works great with Shiitake mushrooms. I like to add a sprinkle of coarse sea salt and vincotto (reduced wine must) for a mix of sweet and salty. It makes a great side dish with grilled meat.

1 pound of Shiitake or other "flat cap" wild mushrooms, wiped clean

Sea salt

1 cup flour

1 large garlic clove cut in half or 2 small cloves

Vincotto or reduced balsamic vinegar *(see instructions on page 11)*

Vegetable oil for frying

Bring a medium sized pot of water to a boil. Add ½ teaspoon of salt. Add the mushrooms and garlic. Once the water returns to a boil remove the mushrooms and garlic. Rinse under cold water, strain and pat dry with paper towels. Season with salt.

Dredge mushrooms in flour. Pan fry in very hot vegetable oil. Drain on paper towel.

Sprinkle with sea salt and drizzle with vincotto or reduced balsamic vinegar.

Yield : 4 appetizers or sides

ZUCCHINI FLOWER FRITTERS

This is a recipe I grew up with and a family favourite! As it is so seasonal, it's something we only enjoy in the summer months. (Substituting grated zucchini in the winter is a great alternative.) If you're lucky to find the blossoms in a market it is much quicker. We grow them and gather them over a number of days. These are best enjoyed right out of the frying pan. They rarely make it to the table.

2 cups zucchini blossoms, washed, blanched *(*See preparation instructions below)*

– OR –

2 cups grated zucchini with peel on *(**See preparation instructions below)*

3 cups flour

1 tsp. salt, plus more for seasoning

⅓ tsp. baking powder

2 ¾ cups water + extra (for extra light fritters use Italian carbonated mineral water and omit salt)

Sea salt, optional

*Pick flowers when they are open, watching for bees and other insects. Two large bowls of zucchini flowers equal roughly 2 cups blanched. I gather my blossoms daily, in the morning over 4-5 days until I have enough. You could also blanch them, cool them off and freeze until you have enough. They are very perishable and don't last long in the fridge. Remove the stem and other green pieces on the cap. Tear gently in 2 pieces and wash. Bring water to a boil and add blossoms. Boil for approximately 1-2 minutes until limp and cooked. Let them cool off. Season blossoms with a little salt.

**Add a generous sprinkle of salt to the grated zucchini in a bowl and let them sit for 20 minutes or so to release the moisture. Squeeze them gently or twist them gently in a tea towel until all the liquid is removed.

In a large bowl mix the flour, 1 teaspoon salt and baking powder. Add water and whisk until no lumps remain.

Add blossoms or grated zucchini to the batter and using your hand mix until all is incorporated and the batter is a light yellow colour. It should be the consistency of thin pancake batter.

Heat ½ inch of vegetable oil in a large non-stick frying pan. When hot, fry about 1/3 cup of batter at a time, spreading it out so it is not too thick (add more water if necessary to thin batter). Cook and turn while frying until golden on both sides (you may have to turn them over a few times). Drain on paper towels, serve hot.

Sprinkle with sea salt if you wish, and enjoy!

Yield: 6-8 Servings

Pizza e Pane
Pizza & Bread

WHAT'S THE DIFFERENCE BETWEEN NORTH AMERICAN AND ITALIAN PIZZA FLOUR?

Ever since I lived in Italy during the 1990s, I've been curious about the differences between North American flour and Italian flour.

In Canada and the U.S., it's fairly simple: we have all purpose flour; bread flour; pastry flour; and whole wheat flour. All purpose has been established to give the home cook good results for just about any dish. It's made from a mix of both hard and soft wheat. On the other hand, to achieve optimal cooking results, you may want to begin using specialty flours, such as bread or pastry.

The percentage of gluten or protein in the flour will change according to the specialized usage. Bread flour is made from hard wheat and has a higher gluten content. This is why it's hard to find gluten-free bread with the same texture as regular bread. Pastry flour is the opposite: it's made from soft wheat and has a lower gluten content. Whole wheat flour is high in fibre, and is usually mixed with other flours. It usually cannot be substituted cup for cup for all purpose flour.

Italian Flour

Italian flour, like other European flours, is categorized differently, on a numerical scale: 2, 1, 0 or 00. This number does not refer to the percentage of gluten or protein in the flour, but rather, to how finely ground it is (2 being the coarsest and 00 being the finest).

Again, the gluten or protein percentage determines how each grade of flour should be used. For example, some flours are best for pasta, bread or pastry. It seems that different manufacturers have different opinions on which is best though.

To sum up, Italian flours allow the cook to choose both the composition (gluten or protein content) and how finely ground the flour is. Italian flour grades are simply more specialized, thereby providing the cook with more choice! It can be confusing for the average cook, but if you can decipher what works best for your recipe, you can achieve a better result.

After living in Italy for close to three years and running my Italian cooking school for nearly seven years, these are what I find work best in my kitchen:

- "00" Farina di Grano Tenero for short rise, thin crust pizza

- "00" Farina di Grano Tenero for gnocchi (it makes them really light)

- Bread Flour mixed with Semola Rimacinata di Grano Duro for focaccia and bread

- All Purpose Flour or Bread Flour mixed with Semola Remacinata di Grano Duro for thick crust pan pizza

- "00" Farina di Grano Tenero mixed with Bread Flour for long rise, thin crust pizza (pizzeria style)

- "00" Farina di Grano Tenero for fresh, egg pasta

- Semola Rimacinata di Grano Duro for eggless, fresh pasta or pasta going through an extruder

I will continue to experiment with different flours until I get the results I want.

I'm always on a quest to cook things that transport me to Italy in one bite, so I've made a habit of visiting the grocery store when I'm in Italy or other North American cities to look for what's new. I encourage you to do the same!

NATALINA'S KITCHEN · BRINGING HOMEMADE BACK

EASY NO-KNEAD FOCACCIA

The Focaccia pictured is Focaccia Barese, typical of Bari, Puglia.
My version here is a quick, no knead recipe. I love the results, even
though it is pretty effortless. It's a great addition to an antipasto
platter or as a snack with a glass of Southern Italian red! Some other
variations include slices of sweet onion or fresh rosemary sprigs. The
classic is just salt and olive oil on top.

1 tsp. traditional yeast

1 ½ cups luke warm water

2 ¾ - 3 cups all purpose or bread flour

1 ½ tsp. salt

2 tbsp. olive oil

1 tbsp. coarse sea salt

Optional: 1 tsp. dried oregano and a pint of cherry or grape tomatoes

Sprinkle yeast over water in a large bowl. Set aside for 5 minutes. Mix thoroughly.

Add flour and salt all at once, stirring with a wooden spoon until the flour is absorbed. Dough should be sticky, not wet. Add more flour if necessary. Cover with plastic wrap, let rest one hour until doubled. Punch down and let rest 10 minutes.

Divide the dough in half and shape into two balls. Use oiled fingers to pat out dough to a dinner plate size on a piece of parchment paper that has been dusted with flour. (It will be rough on top). If using, push the tomatoes into the dough and brush remaining oil on top. Cover again and let rise in a warm place for about 30 minutes.

Preheat oven to 450°F. If using a pizza stone, heat the stone in the oven. After second rise, sprinkle top with sea salt and oregano (if using).

If using a pizza stone use the pizza peel to quickly slide the dough on parchment paper onto the stone, or place on a cookie sheet in the oven.

Bake for 25-30 minutes until golden and the internal temperature is 210°F. Cool on a rack.

Yield: 8-10 Servings

PAN PIZZA WITH BASIL PESTO & CHEESE

Growing up we had homemade pizza and homemade soup every Saturday in the winter. After tobogganing all afternoon, it was nice to come home to those familiar smells.

Homemade pizza is always a treat at my house and this is the quickest one to satisfy a hungry crowd. I can decide on a weeknight at 4 p.m. to make pizza and have this on the table by 5:30 p.m.! I always have yeast, flour and tomato sauce on hand, and often the toppings will be whatever needs to be used up in the fridge. Sure, I love thin crust pizza in my wood-fired oven, but I have to make that dough the day before and the oven needs a lot of tending. This is a quick, pan pizza that when served with a bowl of hearty soup makes a meal.

1 package active, dry yeast *OR* **2 ¼ tsp. loose**

1 cup luke warm water

½ tsp. salt

2 tsp. olive oil

2 ½ cups all-purpose flour *OR* **1 ½ cups bread flour plus 1 cup semolina flour**

Olive oil to grease the pan

1 batch of Pizza Sauce (recipe on page 27)

¼ cup Basil Pesto (recipe on page 45)

3 cups or more shredded mozzarella cheese

Dissolve yeast in warm water in a warm stand mixer bowl. Add salt, olive oil and flour(s). Mix in stand mixer one minute on low speed.

Increase speed slightly and mix until the dough comes away from the sides of the bowl. Knead on speed two for two minutes.

Place dough in greased bowl, turning to coat. Cover, let rise in a warm place until doubled in bulk, approximately 1 hour. Punch dough down.

Grease a cookie sheet or 14-inch pizza pan with oil. Using oiled hands, stretch dough out as evenly as possible. For a thinner crust, go all the way to the edges. For a thicker crust make an oval in the pan that is thicker. Spread desired amount of pizza sauce on the dough and dollop pea-sized portions of pesto on the sauce. Top with the shredded cheese.

Bake at 450°F for 15-20 minutes, or until cooked through.

Yield: 8 Servings

SIMPLE PIZZA SAUCE

Pizza sauce is so simple. If you have pureed tomatoes and a few other ingredients, there is no need to buy pizza sauce. You can double or triple this recipe and freeze for later use.

2 cups tomato puree (passata)

2 tbsp. extra virgin olive oil

¼ tsp. dried oregano

¼ tsp. garlic powder or 1 crushed clove

Salt to taste

Heat oil in saucepan. If using fresh garlic, add the crushed clove. Flavour the oil for a minute, being careful not to brown the garlic. Add tomato puree. Stir and simmer 10 minutes until cooked or oil pools on the top. Add the oregano, garlic powder if using, and salt to taste. Cool slightly before putting on pizza.

Yield: enough for 1 large pan pizza

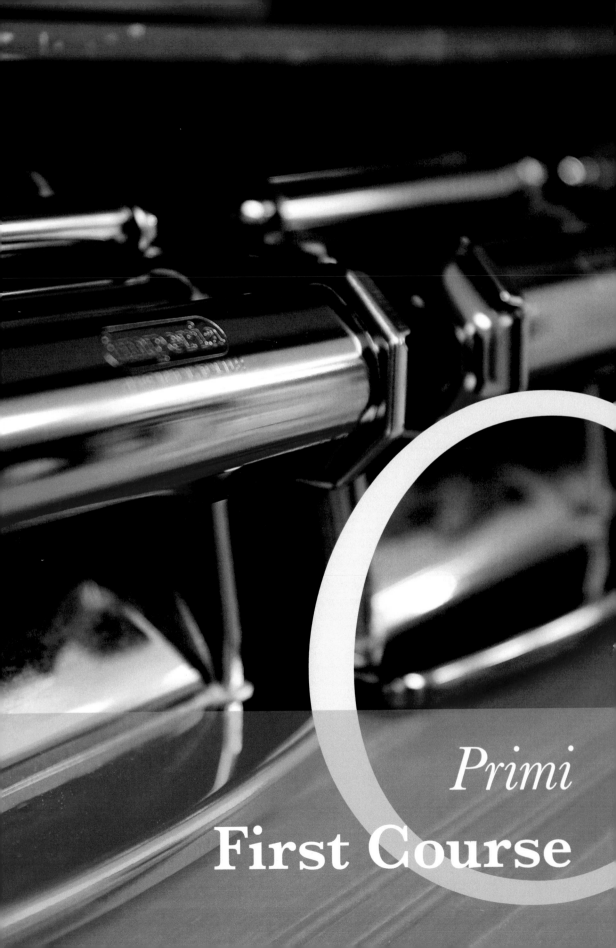

Primi

First Course

COOKING PASTA 101

The fine art of cooking pasta may be the most discussed topic in my kitchen! I witnessed an Italian mamma cooking pasta pretty much every day of my life from birth to adulthood, and the process is almost ingrained in me. All my senses know exactly what it should taste, smell, feel and look like. Travelling and living in Italy strengthened my knowledge and instincts as well. Here are some of the trade secrets that I use every time I make pasta.

First of all, you need to start with good quality pasta. When it comes to dried pasta, I prefer imported Italian pasta. In my experience, Italians just make better pasta, and they have both commercial and artisanal varieties. I would rather use dried Italian pasta than commercially made fresh pasta. If it's fresh pasta, homemade is always better. The expiry date alone on domestic, grocery store pasta tells me there are loads of preservatives in it, which doesn't make good pasta. I don't even need to check the ingredients! Take a class with me if you wish to learn the art of fresh pasta making – it is not as hard as you think.

Secondly, you need a large pot filled with water. To cook 500 grams or 1-pound package of dried pasta, use at least a 5-litre or 4.4-quart pot. Fill the pot at least 80% full and bring to a boil on high heat with the lid on.

Once it comes to a full, rolling boil, I add the salt. In my kitchen it is always added right before adding the pasta so there is never a question as to whether or not anyone added salt. If cooking pasta is the most discussed topic in my school, then how much salt to add to pasta has to be the most controversial! In order for the pasta to be seasoned properly with salt, we have to over-season the water, as most of this salt is going right down the drain when we strain the pasta, and the pasta will only absorb some of the salt. I add a heaping tablespoon of salt to this size pot. The water should taste like sea water to properly season the pasta. If I am using a new or unfamiliar pot, I will taste the water after adding salt. Properly salting the water is one of the fundamentals of cooking pasta. Chefs get sent home in cooking competitions for this all the time!

After salting the water appropriately, add the package of pasta and give it a stir with a wooden spoon, keeping the lid off from now on. Start by setting the timer for the minimum recommended time listed on the package. If you're cooking your own homemade pasta, taste is the best indicator after 1-2 minutes. Stir your pasta occasionally so it doesn't stick, and refrain from adding oil to the water. Good quality pasta will not stick if you stir it occasionally, and oil will prevent your sauce from sticking when dressing the pasta. Begin tasting it once three-quarters of the boiling time has passed.

Taste and mouthfeel are the best indicators of your pasta's progress. You should be able to bite through it easily, but the pasta should still have firmness by the time it's ready. This texture is known as *al dente*, or, in English, "to the tooth". If it has been seasoned properly, the pasta should be flavourful.

Once the pasta is cooked, strain it in a large colander in the sink. I never rinse pasta when I strain it, as the starch helps the sauce adhere, and rinsing cools down the pasta. If you need to keep some of the cooking liquid, keep a heat-proof measuring cup in the sink and fill it before straining the pasta. Either add the pasta back to the pot if your recipe requires further cooking (you may wish to undercook the pasta to compensate for this), or add the pasta to a serving platter with some sauce added to it. Dress the pasta with enough sauce to coat but not drown it, and serve extra sauce on the table for those that prefer more.

Usually, I serve pasta with chillies and cheese added at the table. Enjoy!

FRESH EGG PASTA

Pasta is one of the foundations of Italian cuisine. There are as many fresh pasta recipes as there are Italians! The recipes from Northern Italy tend to have more eggs and egg yolks, therefore making a much richer pasta. The further South you go the less eggs and more water you'll see used in recipes. This is due to the South being a poorer region of the country. There are many hand-formed pastas made with just semola and water in the South – no eggs. They have a different texture and mouthfeel. This is an easy, no fail recipe that I use for fettucine, lasagna and pappardelle.

Per large egg:

1 cup of all purpose flour OR "00" flour for better results

¼ tsp. salt

½ tbsp. olive oil

Water, start by adding 1 tbsp. and add more if needed, to a maximum of 2 tbsp.

Mix flour and salt on the table or board; make a large well in the centre. Crack eggs into well and add oil, 1 tablespoon of water and scramble with a fork.

Start adding a little flour at a time until it is all incorporated.

Knead and add more water if needed until a ball forms. (In humid weather less water will be needed; in dryer temperatures more water will be needed). Don't be tempted to add all the water as a sticky dough will not go through the pasta machine. Continue to knead until smooth dough forms (about 5 minutes).

Cover and let rest, 20-30 minutes.

Form according to your recipe. This dough goes through a pasta machine very easily.

This is a basic recipe. Multiply it according to how many people are being fed. This works really well in a stand mixer with the dough hook or a food processor. Stop it often to touch the texture of the dough and avoid adding too much water.

Yield: 2 first-course portions

RICOTTA & SPINACH STUFFED PASTA SHELLS

These are a crowd pleaser that can be prepared ahead. Make the filling and sauce a day or two ahead. Fill the shells but don't add them to the pan with the sauce until right before baking. If they sit in the sauce for an extended period of time, they will soak up all the sauce and then dry out when baked. These are often on my buffet table as a great vegetarian option and substitute for lasagna. Much easier too!

1 x 475 grams container of ricotta cheese

¼ cup parmesan cheese, extra for sprinkling

1 egg, lightly beaten

¼ cup chopped parsley

Salt

⅛ tsp. pepper

½ cup mozzarella cheese

4 cups fresh spinach

1 tbsp. olive oil

1 small onion, diced

Dash nutmeg

1 batch Tomato Basil Sauce made with pureed tomatoes (see recipe on page 51)

22 dry pasta shells

Bring a large pot of water to boil. Add 1 tablespoon of salt and add the pasta shells. Undercook by 2 minutes according to instructions on package. Run under cool water. Strain water.

Meanwhile, heat olive oil in a frying pan. Add onion and sauté a few minutes until limp. Add spinach and coat with oil. Add a pinch of salt and a dash of nutmeg, and cook until limp. Remove from heat and cool.

Mix ricotta, parmesan, parsley, ½ teaspoon salt, pepper, and mozzarella in a bowl. Chop cooled spinach and add to filling. Taste, adjusting salt and pepper. Add beaten egg. Preheat oven to 350°F.

Add filling to each each shell. Add 1 cup of water to the tomato basil sauce to thin it out. Place a generous amount of sauce (½ inch) in the bottom of an oven-safe dish or pan. Place the shells in one layer on the sauce and top with a little more sauce. Sprinkle parmesan cheese.

Cover with tin foil. Bake until the sauce is bubbling and the filling is hot when tested with a knife, about 40 minutes.

Yield: 4-6 Servings

CLASSIC POTATO GNOCCHI

Gnocchi are everyone's favourite! My mother never made them, as they are not typical of the South. My Aunt used to make them at my Nonna's, but we had to eat in shifts as they are not conducive to large crowds!

One of my most requested classes was potato gnocchi with braised beef and roasted root vegetables. Use the sauce from the beef to dress the gnocchi, and serve the gnocchi as your starch alongside the beef and vegetables! A great Winter menu for a crowd.

4 large russet potatoes with skin on (about 3 lbs.; old, starchy potatoes are best)

3 cups all-purpose flour OR Italian "00" flour + 1 cup for dusting

2 large eggs, slightly beaten with 1 tsp. salt

Scrub the potatoes and boil in large pot with cold water until you can easily insert a knife through the middle. Peel the potatoes while they are still hot, and using either a food mill, ricer or grater, process them directly on a large cookie sheet. Spread out to cool.

Beat the eggs with the salt in a small bowl. Scatter the beaten egg and salt over the potatoes when they are cool. Sprinkle 3 cups of flour over the potatoes. First gently toss all the ingredients to distribute them. Gently start bringing the dough together into a long tube, being careful not to overwork. Cut randomly through the dough and make sure there is no dry flour remaining. Slice off 1 inch of the dough.

Roll into long tubes, about ½ inch thick, on a lightly floured board. Cut ½ inch pieces, press and roll off the end of a fork or gnocchi board to create the shape. Place gently on a cookie sheet with a dusting of flour. Do not stack.

Bring a large pot of boiling water to a boil. Add 1 tablespoon of salt and add some of the gnocchi. This recipe should be cooked in 1-3 batches. Boil approximately 1-2 minutes, or until they rise to the top. Remove gently with a slotted spoon to a colander to continue to strain. Place in a warmed bowl while you boil the rest in batches.

Add a little sauce and toss gently so they don't stick. Serve immediately with your favourite sauce.

Yield: 8-10 people

PASTA WITH RAPINI AND FRESH RICOTTA

I love this dish. It is very simple so the best ingredients are very important here. I developed it one day when I opened the fridge and I had some beautiful fresh ricotta and rapini that needed to be used up. The finishing drizzle of the best extra virgin olive oil is very important here... it really makes this dish! Some crusty bread comes in handy too to soak up the leftovers on the plate!

Fresh Pasta Fettuccine, made with 2 eggs (see recipe on page 31) *OR* 1 lb. dry pasta

1 bunch fresh rapini, cleaned and blanched in boiling water until large stems yield to pressure, and cooled, rough chopped

¼ cup virgin olive oil

3 garlic cloves, crushed

1 tsp. crushed chillies or more (optional)

Salt/fresh ground black pepper

1 cups fresh ricotta cheese, preferably good quality, fresh

Good quality Extra virgin olive oil for finishing

Heat ¼ cup of olive oil in a large frying pan. Add garlic and sauté until fragrant, not brown. Add rapini and coat with oil. Heat rapini thoroughly. Add salt and chillies to taste. Set aside.

Bring a large pot of water to boil. Add 1 tablespoon salt and add pasta. Cook until al dente. Drain the pasta reserving 1 cup of the cooking liquid.

Add the pasta to the frying pan and coat thoroughly with oil and rapini. Add 2 tablespoons of the water to the pan and mix it all together until a nice consistency is reached, adding more water if necessary. Taste for seasoning.

Serve each portion with a ¼ cup of ricotta on top. Season the ricotta with salt and fresh ground pepper and a drizzle of good quality olive oil.

Yield: 4 Servings

RISOTTO – WILD MUSHROOM

Risotto is one of my favourite dishes to teach and eat! My mother, being of Southern Italian origin, never made it as it is a typical northern Italian dish. When my own family moved to Milano in 1997, I ate it often and developed a love for the dish. I asked my husband's Italian teacher, Sonia, to come to our home one evening and teach me to make it. When she arrived I had homemade stock simmering on the stove and the children were eating a home-cooked meal at the table. She gave me a compliment I will always cherish: "you are Canadian, but your kitchen is Italian!"

2 cups Arborio *OR* Carnaroli rice

6 cups homemade or good quality chicken stock (no salt or reduced salt)

1 cup fresh mushrooms

20 grams *OR* 0.7 ounces dry wild mushrooms

¼ cup unsalted butter, in pieces

½ cup parmesan cheese

¼ cup virgin olive oil

2 small shallots, minced

½ cup dry white wine

Soak dry mushrooms in 1 cup of boiling water 10-15 minutes. Remove mushrooms, save liquid.

Bring the stock to a boil, add the reserved mushroom liquid pouring through a strainer first. Reduce heat to a simmer.

Meanwhile in a hot, heavy-bottomed pot with a large surface area, heat the oil on medium high heat. Add all the mushrooms and shallots and sauté. When limp and fragrant, add the rice. Coat the rice in the oil and "toast the rice" for a few minutes. Deglaze with the wine. Stir and let it evaporate. Reduce heat to medium. Add 2 ladles of stock. Keep stirring constantly with a flat wooden spoon until most of the stock is absorbed. Continue to add 1 ladle of stock at a time, stirring constantly. Continue until all but a couple of ladles of stock remain. Taste the rice. It should be almost cooked, but still quite firm.

Add the butter and the parmesan cheese. Stir until incorporated and the butter is melted. Add salt and pepper to taste and 1 more ladle of stock. The rice should be fully cooked now but still *al dente*. Risotto should move on the plate when served, so add more stock if needed to achieve this before serving.

Yield: 4-6 Servings

RISOTTO – ASPARAGUS

Another classic risotto dish with asparagus. I enjoy this in the spring when asparagus is plentiful. I prefer risotto at room temperature, not piping hot, so this is still a great dish as the weather gets warmer!

1 lb. asparagus, washed and chopped into 1 inch pieces

3 cups homemade or good quality chicken OR vegetable stock (no or reduced salt)

3 tbsp. of olive oil

2 tbsp. unsalted butter

1 small shallot, diced (unsalted)

2 cups Arborio rice

Salt and ground black pepper

½ cup parmesan cheese

Bring a medium pot of water to boil. Add asparagus, and blanch for 3-4 minutes. Keep the boiling liquid by removing the asparagus with a slotted spoon and rinsing it under cold water to stop cooking. Set blanched tips aside. Measure out 3¾ cups of the asparagus cooking water and return to pot with stock and heat until simmering.

In a large heavy-bottomed pot, heat the olive oil. Add shallots and sauté until soft and golden. Add the asparagus (not the tips) and sauté for 2-3 minutes. Add the rice, stirring to coat. Toast for a few minutes.

Over medium heat, stir in a ladle full of stock and stir with a wooden spoon until completely absorbed. Continue adding stock 1 ladle at a time and stirring until each evaporates. Continue to do this until the rice is *al dente* and some stock remains. Remove from heat and add the asparagus tips, remaining butter and parmesan cheese. Taste and adjust seasoning with salt and pepper. Add more stock if needed to achieve a loose consistency.

Yield: 4-6 Servings

RISOTTO – SQUASH

This is a lovely fall risotto when squash is in season. You could substitute any kind of squash, but butternut is my favourite. The sage, butter, squash and parmesan cheese are a classic flavour combination used in northern Italy quite often. It is comfort food at it's best!

4 cups of homemade or good quality chicken OR vegetable stock (no or reduced salt), plus 2 cups of water

4 cups butternut squash, chopped into ½ inch cubes

2 tbsp. olive oil

1 small shallot, minced

2 tbsp. fresh sage, minced

Salt & pepper to taste

2 cups Arborio rice

¼ cup dry white wine

½ cup parmesan cheese

1 tbsp. unsalted butter

Bring 2 cups of water and stock to a boil in a medium-sized pot. Reduce to simmer.

Add the squash and cook 3 minutes; remove with a slotted spoon. Meanwhile heat the oil in a heavy-bottomed pot. Add the shallots and sweat. Once the shallots are fragrant and translucent, add the rice and coat with oil. Toast the rice for 2 minutes. Add the squash and sauté 1 minute. Add the wine and deglaze the pan.

Add the stock gradually, 1 ladle at a time until it is absorbed. Continue to do this until just 2 ladles remain. Add the sage, cheese and butter. Season to taste; adjust consistency with more stock if necessary. It should be loose on the plate when served.

Yield: 4-6 Servings

BASIL PESTO

Basil pesto is something I always have on hand. It freezes well so when we have an abundance of basil from our garden this is a great way to store it. When I don't have fresh basil on hand for a tomato sauce it is a great substitute. My kids use it like a condiment on sandwiches. My favourite is grilled chicken, basil pesto and provolone cheese in a pressed panini... Yum!

2 ½ cups packed fresh basil leaves (tender leaves only), washed and air-dried

½ cup extra virgin olive oil

¼ cup pine nuts

3 garlic cloves, minced

¼ tsp. salt

½ cup grated parmesan cheese

2 tbsp. grated Pecorino Romano cheese

Process all ingredients, except the cheeses, in a food processor. Stir in cheeses by hand. Store covered in fridge for up to 1 week. Makes about 1¼ cups of pesto.

When using with pasta, be sure to save some of the pasta cooking water and mix in to get a velvety consistency.

Makes enough for 1 pound of pasta.

Yield: 4-6 Servings

SAUCE WITH MEATBALLS & SAUSAGE

Meatballs! My family's favourite comfort meal. This was often a Sunday lunch in my childhood home. We always had to eat our pasta first, before having the meatballs that were served as a second course. This was often a lesson in patience as we waited for everyone to finish their pasta! This is my original Calabrese family recipe that poaches the meatballs directly in the sauce without browning them first. They are moister and the meatballs flavour the sauce.

1 pound ground meat (preferably a mix of lean ground beef, pork & veal)

4 links of Italian sausage, cut in half

½ cup parmesan cheese, grated

1 large egg

1 cup stale bread, submerged in water to soak

1 tsp. salt

½ tsp. pepper

2 x 680 ml bottles pureed tomatoes

½ cup olive oil

1 handful fresh basil, rolled and chopped

Salt/pepper

1 medium onion, minced

2 tbsp. wine

Heat a heavy-bottomed pot on high heat and add the olive oil. Add the Italian sausage. Brown the sausage in batches and remove from the pot. Add the chopped onion and sweat the onions until fragrant and translucent. Deglaze the pan with the wine and scrape up the brown bits on the bottom of the pot. Reduce the wine by half and then add the tomatoes, plus rinse out each bottle with ½ cup of water. Bring the sauce to a boil and then immediately turn the heat down to simmer gently, with the lid partially open to let the steam escape.

Meanwhile, place the ground meat in a large bowl and season with salt and pepper. Remove the bread from the soaking water, do not squeeze out all the water, tear into small pieces, and add to the meat. Add the cheese and the egg and mix with your hands. Combine thoroughly. Mixture will be wetter than you expect.

Roll 1 ball tightly into the size of ping pong ball and drop it into the simmering sauce to test it. See if it stays together. If it is too loose or does not hold together, add ¼ cup of breadcrumbs and roll them all into balls now. Add a cup of water to the sauce and bring to a boil. Add the meatballs, being careful not to squish them. Shake the pot gently if you need to redistribute them. Reduce the heat to simmer and simmer gently with the lid partially on. DO NOT STIR UNTIL THE MEATBALLS ARE SET, ABOUT 5 MINUTES. Carefully stir, allowing the meatballs to cook and the sauce to reduce, about 15-20 minutes.

Add the sausage back to the pot to continue cooking. After 15-20 minutes the oil should start to pool on top. This is an indicator that it is ready. Add ¼ teaspoon of salt and ¼ teaspoon of ground black pepper and the basil. Stir, taste and adjust the seasonings.

Yield: 4-6 Servings

GROUND MEAT & TOMATO SAUCE

This is a very simple ground meat and tomato sauce, not to be confused with Bolognese sauce. Bolognese sauce is mostly meat with just a bit of tomato and is typically a mix of veal, pork and pancetta. I often use this with a short pasta such as penne or rigatoni.

1 pound ground meat (preferably a mix of lean ground beef, pork & veal)

1 medium onion, diced

¼ cup olive oil

2 tbsp. wine

1 x 680 ml bottle pureed tomatoes

Fresh basil

Salt & pepper

1½ lbs. dry pasta

Heat a heavy-bottomed saucepan on medium-high heat. Add olive oil and heat until hot.

Add ground meat and break up with a spoon. Brown the meat until no longer pink. Add onions and sweat until fragrant and soft. Deglaze pan with wine and scrape off any brown bits on the pan. Cook until wine is translucent and oil is clear.

Add pureed tomatoes and add about 1/3 cup of water in the bottle and rinse out the remaining tomato. Bring to a boil, and immediately turn the heat down to simmer until sauce is reduced and thickened, about 45 minutes to 1 hour. Stir occasionally.

Sauce is ready when the oil is "pools" on top. Add salt and pepper. Taste and adjust seasoning. Add a handful of torn basil. Serve over your favourite pasta with parmesan cheese and chillies!

Yield: 6 Servings

TOMATO BASIL SAUCE

This is my family's recipe and a great example of simple Italian cooking. Only four ingredients plus seasoning means the ingredients should be the finest in quality. Read my tips on tomatoes (page 61) and olive oil (page 93) to learn how to choose the best. I use this recipe often and switch up the tomatoes and the seasonings to adapt it. In this cookbook, it is used 3 different ways. A versatile sauce that freezes well, my students tell me they will never buy prepared sauce again!

¼ cup virgin olive oil

1 x 28 fl. oz. tin of whole peeled tomatoes, crushed by hand

OR

1 x 680 ml bottle of pureed tomato (I use the pureed tomato for baked dishes)

1 medium onion *OR* ½ medium onion and 1 shallot, chopped

Handful of fresh basil, rolled and sliced

Salt/pepper to taste

In a hot medium-sized pot, add oil. When hot (not smoking), add onions and shallots on medium-high heat. Sweat until fragrant and translucent, stirring occasionally

Add crushed tomatoes or pureed tomato, stir and bring to a boil. Once it comes to a boil, reduce the temperature to a simmer. Place the lid on the pot with a small vent left open.

Reduce the sauce until desired consistency is reached, stirring occasionally. Add salt/pepper and basil.

Stir, taste and adjust seasonings.

Yield: 4-6 Servings

MILANESE MINESTRONE SOUP WITH RICE

Minestrone is a classic Italian soup. The different regions of Italy have their own versions based on what is available in the area. When I lived in Milano for a few years I came to love their adaptation with rice. This is my version. The little bits of pancetta add an interesting texture and you could easily substitute any leafy green for the swiss chard... spinach or kale maybe?

¼ cup olive oil

½ cup diced pancetta

1 medium onion

1 leek

2 medium carrots

2 stalks of celery

⅛ medium cabbage

1 bunch swiss chard

4 plum tomatoes

2 litres of homemade or good quality stock, heated

½ cup white *OR* red kidney beans

¾ cup of long grain rice, partially cooked

¼ cup of tomato paste

Fresh herbs such as thyme *OR* 5-6 basil leaves (chopped)

2 bay leaves

Salt

Pepper

Parmesan cheese to sprinkle on top

Dice all the vegetables into similar size. Separate the stems of the swiss chard from the leaves. Chop tomatoes.

Add the oil to a large , heavy-bottomed pot. Heat until simmering. Add the pancetta and sauté until the fat is rendered and it is golden. Add the onions and continue without browning.

Add all the vegetables except the leaves of the chard and plum tomatoes and continue to sweat. The vegetables should be limp and fragrant. Add the tomato paste, stir and let it caramelize a bit before adding the chopped tomatoes. Mix well. Add the stock and deglaze the pot. Bring to a boil, reduce heat to simmer and skim off impurities.

Add the rice, beans, herbs, and chard leaves. Simmer 5-10 minutes until blended and season with salt and pepper. Taste and adjust seasonings. Serve with parmesan cheese.

This freezes well without the rice. Add rice when reheating.

Yield: 8-10 Servings

PASTA E FAGIOLI SOUP

Pasta fagioli is a one of those dishes that reminds me of my childhood. It is simple Italian cooking at it's best. Again, because of the simplicity, the ingredients you choose make a big difference. We grow and dry our own Borlotti beans. The next best choice would be to buy dried beans, soak them, and boil them according to the directions on the package. Lastly, canned beans can work in a pinch.

1 cup of dry Romano *OR* Borlotti beans soaked overnight and boiled according to package directions, reserving the boiling liquid

OR

One 28 fl. oz. tin of good quality Italian canned Romano *OR* Borlotti beans and the liquid

¼ cup good quality Italian olive oil

14 oz. good quality Italian hand-crushed plum tomatoes (San Marzano or Romano)

Water

Salt to taste

1 lb. good quality Italian short pasta such as ditali or small shells

A large handful of fresh basil, chopped in shreds

Bring a large pot of water to a boil. Add 1 tablespoon of salt and add the pasta.

Meanwhile in a medium-sized pot, add the olive oil, beans and liquid and crushed tomatoes. Add enough water to the pot to just cover the ingredients. Stir and bring to a boil over medium-high heat. Stir and reduce heat to simmer. Simmer with the lid partially on, until thickened and reduced. Once broth is thickened, reduced and the beans are fully cooked, add the chopped basil.

Continue cooking the pasta until a few minutes short of being fully cooked. Save 2 cups of the pasta cooking water and strain the pasta.

Add the cooked pasta, the bean sauce and 1 cup of the cooking water to the broth in large pot. Mix and bring to a boil. Reduce the temperature to simmer and add salt to taste. Let the sauce thicken and the flavours blend together. Add more of the cooking liquid if needed to make a soup-like consistency. Add more chopped basil and adjust the salt if needed. Drizzle with extra virgin olive oil. Serve with crusty bread for dunking in the sauce.

Yield: 4-6 Servings

SOUP – PASTA WITH BROCCOLI

My daughter's favourite pasta! This is a dish I grew up with and is a perfect example of "la cucina povera". This soup has only a few ingredients, and yet when you use the freshest broccoli and the best olive oil, you have a quick and easy soup that can even be served to guests.

1 bunch fresh broccoli, washed and cut into 1 inch pieces

¼ cup virgin olive oil

½ cup pureed tomatoes

¾ pound farfalle or pasta shells

Salt

Crushed chili peppers

1 large clove garlic, crushed or chopped

Good quality extra virgin olive oil to finish

Bring a large pot of water to a boil. Add broccoli, pasta and 1 tablespoon salt. Stir.

Meanwhile, heat the oil in a small saucepan and sauté garlic until fragrant, not brown. Add the pureed tomato and bring to a boil; reduce to simmer. Cook until the oil separates, only a few minutes.

When the pasta is slightly undercooked and the broccoli is cooked, pour out some of the water into a 2 cup measuring cup, leaving only enough to cover pasta and broccoli.

Return pot to the burner and add sauce, removing garlic if desired. Stir and simmer until thickened. Add salt to taste. Add more of the pasta water if needed to reach a thick, soup-like consistency. Check and adjust seasoning. Serve with a sprinkle of chillies and a drizzle of the best extra virgin olive oil.

Yield: 4-6 Servings

ITALIAN TURKEY MEATBALL SOUP WITH SPINACH

This Italian-inspired soup eats like a meal as it has lots of protein, vegetables, and rice. It comes together pretty quickly if you use a ready-made prepared stock. Just add a salad and you have a complete meal.

For meatballs:

1 pound lean, ground turkey

1 tsp. salt

½ tsp. black ground pepper

½ cup fine, plain breadcrumbs

½ cup grated parmesan cheese

1 egg

¼ cup of water

For soup:

2 tablespoons olive oil

2 carrots, chopped

1 celery stalk, chopped

1 medium onion, chopped

1 ½ tablespoons of tomato paste

1 cup of dry rice (white, brown or wild) cooked, but not fully

¼ tsp. dry thyme or 1 tablespoon fresh, chopped thyme

½ tbsp. salt (you may not need this if there is salt in the stock)

½ tsp. ground black pepper

5 oz. (4 cups) trimmed, washed baby spinach or kale leaves

1 ½ liters homemade or good quality chicken stock (no or reduced salt)

Method: Meatballs

Preheat the oven to 400°F. Mix all the meatball ingredients in a bowl until combined well. Form into 12 large meatballs or 24 medium-sized meatballs. Place on a cookie sheet with parchment paper or a silicon sheet. Bake until internal temperature reaches about 65°C, almost fully cooked.

Method: Soup

While you are baking the meatballs, heat the olive oil in a large, heavy-bottomed pot. Add the carrots, celery, and onion. Sweat until fragrant and translucent, not brown, about 5 minutes. Add the tomato paste and mix in until it becomes deep in color, might stick to the bottom of the pot. Add the chicken stock and bring to a boil. Add the partially cooked rice. Add the meatballs, thyme, salt (only if the stock is low salt/salt-free) and pepper. Continue on simmer until the rice and meatballs are fully cooked (71°C internal temperature) and the flavours have blended. Taste and adjust seasonings. Add the spinach and stir until wilted.

Serve with grated parmesan cheese. Enjoy!

Yield: 6 Servings

Secondi

Second Course

CANNED TOMATOES: THE GOOD, THE NOT-SO-BAD AND THE UGLY

Canned tomatoes are a staple in my kitchen. Contrary to popular belief fresh are not always better. Actually, where I live in in Canada, fresh are only better in the late summer and – if we're lucky – into fall.

We grow many varieties in our large, backyard garden and I enjoy them daily when they are in season. I often preserve tomatoes from my garden in a variety of ways. I can whole, plum tomatoes, and I also make my own passata, or pureed tomatoes, from the backyard bounty.

However, I could never rely solely on the tomatoes from my garden to supply both my own kitchen and my busy Italian cooking school, so I often buy canned and bottled tomatoes by the case.

My students always ask me how to choose the right tomatoes. The answer is always: buy the ones with the fewest ingredients. In other words, the ingredient list should consist of tomatoes, maybe salt, maybe basil, but that's all. Citric acid is a common ingredient in canned tomatoes, and it's unnecessary.

Next, when you're buying canned tomatoes, consider the variety. Plum is the most common, and San Marzano is the best-tasting (that is, if they are real San Marzanos – more about that below!) Plum tomatoes were actually developed for canning. They are firm with few seeds, they peel easily, and they are pretty meaty. In short, they are a great all-purpose tomato that can be used in many ways. I buy Italian plum tomatoes by the case, and these canned tomatoes contain only tomatoes and salt. It's important to note that the salt in Italian plum tomatoes is not added, as the Italian tomatoes naturally contain more salt than Canadian ones because they are grown on a small peninsula surrounded by salt water. I use them for sauces, quick soups, and other tomato-based dishes.

I also use Canadian-grown Roma tomatoes. They are not as sweet, usually contain more seeds, and are not as plump, so I use them in dishes where the tomatoes are just one of many ingredients, such as in a stew or soup.

If you're wondering about the authenticity of San Marzanos, let me provide you with a little history.

San Marzano is a variety of tomato that is grown in the rich, volcanic soil of Mount Vesuvius, near Naples. It is a beautifully rich, sweet tomato with very few seeds, and in order for it to be a true San Marzano, it must be grown there, and must have the DOP symbol (the gold-coloured seal of approval), along with a serial number. When you see a vendor at a farmer's market selling fresh tomatoes, it's very unlikely that those tomatoes are San Marzanos (unless you live near Mount Vesuvius, of course!).

Now, when it comes to authentic San Marzanos, where should you use them? I use them when tomatoes are the star ingredient, and there are very few other ingredients complementing it. For example, I use San Marzanos on a thin-crust margherita pizza, or in a simple tomato basil sauce served over fresh pasta. Use them where you will certainly appreciate them and know they are special, along with other authentic, Italian ingredients!

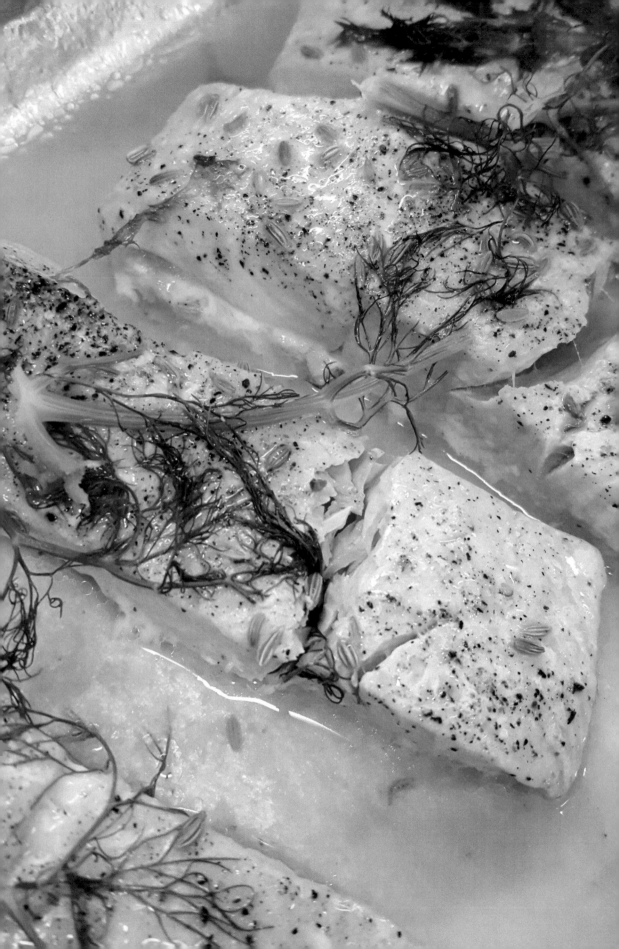

BAKED SALMON WITH FENNEL

Seafood in Italy is very abundant and is usually prepared in a way that the seafood is the star. In other words, very simply prepared. This recipe was adapted to salmon in my classes, as it is a common fish in Canada and readily availble. In Italy this would be prepared with a typical fish of the region, such as sea bass. One whole fish per person would be served and the cavity would be stuffed with the fennel fronds and seasonings. The fennel gives it a very mild flavouring that still allows the fresh fish to shine!

Salmon fillet *OR* 4 salmon portions

Salt

Ground black pepper

¼ cup dry white wine

⅛ cup extra virgin olive oil

1 tsp. fennel seeds

Fresh fennel fronds

Place a large sheet of tin foil on a cookie sheet (enough to come up and tent the fish). Drizzle a small amount of olive oil on the foil, and place the salmon on top. Season with salt and pepper. Sprinkle fennel seeds and place fronds on top. Drizzle remaining oil on the salmon. Pour white wine on top.

Bring up the sides of the foil to "tent" and seal the foil tightly. Bake in a 450°F oven for 10 minutes per one inch of fillet thickness (typically 10-12 minutes). Fish should flake when ready. Do not overcook.

Yield: 4 Servings

CHICKEN *OR* VEAL PARMIGIANA

This is a simple recipe I serve often to my family. It is great alongside pasta, using the sauce to dress the pasta, or with potatoes and vegetables. My kids usually fight over the leftovers so it can make an appearance in their lunch box the next day on a crusty roll.

Tomato Basil Sauce, made with whole tomatoes (see recipe on page 51)

½ tsp. dried oregano

2½ cups dried breadcrumbs

2 tbsp. + ¼ cup parmesan cheese

2 eggs

2 tbsp. milk

1 cup flour

Salt/pepper

4 boneless skinless chicken breasts

1 cup grated mozzarella cheese

Vegetable oil for frying

Prepare sauce as instructed, adding oregano with the basil. Let cool a little and, using an immersion blender, puree the sauce. Add 1 cup of water to the sauce to compensate for the reduction in the oven.

Butterfly each chicken breast and divide into 2 pieces. Pound each piece between 2 pieces of plastic wrap until an even consistency of about ½ inch is reached.

Prepare a dredging station in 3 shallow containers. Add flour to the first container. Beat the eggs with the milk in the second container. Add bread crumbs plus 2 tablespoons of parmesan cheese in the third container.

Season chicken with salt and pepper on both sides. Dredge in flour, then egg and milk and finally bread crumbs mixture. Place the chicken cutlets on a platter. Preheat the oven to 350°F.

In a hot frying pan, add ½ inch vegetable oil. Heat oil and add a bread crumb to check the temperature; it should sizzle when ready. Start adding the chicken about 4 cutlets at a time. Only fry the chicken until the coating is slightly golden (the chicken will not be cooked completely). Continue browning all the chicken in batches and place the fried chicken cutlets on a cookie sheet with paper towel to absorb the oil.

Ladle ½ inch of the sauce into an oven safe casserole dish. Lay the chicken on top, overlapping slightly. Spoon more sauce on top. Top with parmesan and mozzarella cheese.

Cover with aluminum foil and bake for approximately 20-25 minutes until the sauce is bubbling and the cheese is melted.

Yield: 4-6 Servings

EGGPLANT PARMIGIANA

If you have vegetarians in the family this is a great dish to make when others are having the meat version. It's not a lot of effort to make this as well. Personally I love it and I am not vegetarian! This is a dish found in the south of Italy and it is the "Original Parmigiana". You'll find it on many menus there.

1 batch of chunky Tomato Basil Sauce (see recipe on page 51)

½ tsp. Italian oregano

2 large or 4 medium eggplants

2 cups grated mozzarella cheese

2 eggs, beaten

½ cup grated parmesan cheese

Flour

Salt

Vegetable oil for frying

Slice the eggplants with the skin on into rounds about ½ inch thick. Season generously with salt and layer in a colander placed in the sink. Let this sit for 20-30 minutes. The bitter liquid will be released. Gently squeeze and pat dry with paper towel.

Dip eggplant slices in flour and coat evenly. Next dip them in the beaten eggs, and fry in hot vegetable oil until golden. Drain on paper towel.

Puree the tomato sauce when cooled and add the oregano. Add ½ cup of water to thin down the sauce. Add ample sauce to the bottom of a baking dish to cover it. Layer the eggplant, overlapping slightly. Spoon the sauce over top and sprinkle both cheeses.

Cover tightly with aluminum foil and bake in a preheated 400°F oven for approximately 20 minutes, or until the sauce is bubbling and the cheese is melted. Remove the foil for the last few minutes of baking and allow the cheese to cook to a golden colour.

Yield: 4-6 servings

ITALIAN BRAISED BEEF IN RED WINE WITH WILD MUSHROOMS

Italian braised beef or Brasato is comfort food at its best. One of my favorite winter dishes, this could be served with pasta or gnocchi with the sauce used to dress the noodles. It would also work well with mashed potatoes or polenta and a side of vegetables. Our most popular menu at the cooking school features this dish as the star (find the full menu on page 127). Enjoy!

Beef blade roast, 2-3 pounds, cubed

¼ cup diced pancetta

2 tbsp. olive oil + more

2 tbsp. canola oil + more

2 cloves of garlic, minced

1 med. onion, diced

1 celery stalk, diced

1 carrot, diced

Flour

1 tbsp. tomato paste

1 cup tomato passata

1 bay leaf/ fresh herbs

1 cup red wine

2 cups of beef stock

¼ cup dried porcini soaked in a 1 cup of boiling water

2 cups sliced cremini mushrooms

Salt/pepper

This recipe requires a large, heavy-bottomed pot with a tight-fitting lid that can go in the oven. Season the cubes of beef with salt and pepper. Dust lightly in flour. In the heated pot, add the pancetta and melt the fat. Remove the pancetta when it is golden. Add the olive oil and canola oil, and heat thoroughly. Add the beef and brown/sear in batches until nice and brown. Remove the beef to a plate. Add the onions, celery, carrots, garlic. Sweat them until fragrant and limp, not brown. Add the tomato paste and heat thoroughly. Deglaze the pot with the wine and scrape up all the brown bits. Reduce wine by a half. Add the tomato passata and the herbs of choice. Add the stock and the liquid from the dry mushrooms (strain through a sieve to remove sediment). Bring to a boil. Add the beef and pancetta back to the pot. The liquid should always come up three quarters of the side of the beef or more.

Secure the lid and put in a preheated 350°F degree oven for 2½ to 3 hours. A ½ hour before the beef is ready, sauté the mushrooms in a hot pan with a dash of olive oil and add to the beef. The beef should be fall-apart tender when ready. Skim off any accumulated fat off the top. Taste, season with salt and pepper, and adjust.

Yield: 4-6 Servings

ITALIAN MARINATED FLANK STEAK

Flank steak is a great, economical dish. This could be done ahead, placed in the fridge and then just grilled before serving. I like to serve this with simple grilled vegetables and roasted potatoes!

¼ **cup olive oil**

⅓ **cup balsamic vinegar**

2 cloves garlic, minced

2 tbsp. chives, minced

1 tbsp. dried oregano

1 tbsp. crushed chili peppers or to taste

2 tbsp. sugar

5 sundried tomatoes, chopped finely

Pinch salt/pepper

1 medium to large flank steak

¼ **cup of beef stock**

For best results, add first nine ingredients to a food processor and process. Once processed, add to a large zip top bag.

Score the flank steak on both sides, careful not to cut right through. Season with salt and pepper. Add the steak to the bag and coat with marinade on both sides.

Refrigerate for 4-6 hours.

Preheat a grill to high. Grill on hot grill until meat is cooked to medium. Remove at 155°F internal temperature. Keep the remaining marinade.

Let rest for 15 minutes while tented with foil.

Add some stock to the bag and shake it to get the marinade to pour out of the bag and into a small pot. Bring to a boil and then down to a simmer. Add more stock or reduce until you have a nice consistency.

Slice thinly across the grain and serve with sauce.

Yield: 4-6 Servings

MEAT STUFFED EGGPLANT

My family grows and cooks a lot of eggplant. It is a common vegetable in the south of Italy, so we have many ways to prepare it. This is one of my favourites! When you place it in the oven you could add some tomato sauce, parmesan cheese and mozzarella cheese. Served over pasta it is delicious!

4 small Italian eggplants (pear-sized)

1 pound ground meat (mixture of ⅓ lean veal, ⅓ lean beef, ⅓ lean pork)

½ tsp. salt

¼ tsp. pepper

¾ cup parmesan cheese

1 cup stale bread covered in water to soak

1 egg

¼ cup fresh parsley, chopped fine

Cut the stem off the eggplant and slice in half lengthwise.

Bring a large pot of water to a boil. Add eggplant and blanch until fork tender. Drain and let cool slightly.

Meanwhile, in a large bowl, add meat, salt, pepper, and cheese. Squeeze out most of the water from the bread, and pull it into small pieces. Add to the stuffing.

When the eggplant has cooled, scoop out all the pulp being careful not to tear the remaining skin. Chop the pulp finely and add to stuffing mix. Add the parsley and the egg. Combine with your hands until evenly mixed. It will seem quite wet. If too wet add a handful of breadcrumbs.

Test a small amount in a frying pan to check seasoning. Stuff the skin "cups". Do not overfill.

If you have stuffing left, shape into a similar shape to the eggplant, about a ½ cup each. Preheat the oven to 350° F.

In a hot non-stick frying pan, heat 1/3 inch vegetable oil. Fry on either side only until brown, being careful when turning. (I use 2 forks and only turn once a crust has formed) Place in a casserole dish and bake covered until fully cooked, about 20 minutes.

Makes about 12-15.

Yield: 4-6 Servings

VEAL *OR* CHICKEN MARSALA
WITH SAGE & MUSHROOMS

Classic veal marsala is a quick and easy dish that could be served to guests. My rendition has the addition of sage. The sage goes well with the butter and Marsala, and who can resist crispy sage as a garnish? You could do everything ahead and then finish the chicken in the oven while you reheat the mushrooms and sauce.

1 lb. veal scallops *OR* 4 chicken breasts

Salt and pepper

¾ cup flour

6-8 tbsp. unsalted butter

3 cups mushrooms sliced

¾ cup dry Marsala wine

2 small bunches of fresh sage leaves, washed and dried

3-4 tbsp. unsalted butter

If using chicken, slice the breasts in half horizontally. For both chicken or veal, pound the meat to even thickness, about ½ inch. Season with salt and pepper.

Dredge in flour lightly. Preheat the oven to 400° F.

Place a large frying pan over medium-high heat and add 3 tablespoons butter. Once melted, fry half of the sage leaves until crispy. Do not overcook. Drain on paper towel.

In the same pan, brown the meat in batches, adding more butter as needed. Do not fully cook! Place on a cookie sheet. Place in the preheated oven for 10-15 minutes to finish cooking.

Meanwhile, add the rest of the butter, the mushrooms and the rest of the sage leaves to the pan. Season with salt and pepper. Cook until tender and moisture has evaporated. Remove the mushrooms and sage, and reserve.

Return the pan to heat and add the Marsala, reducing to about 3-4 tablespoons.

Place the chicken on a platter, spoon the mushrooms on top and then pour the sauce on top. Garnish with the crispy sage.

Yield: 4-6 Servings

Contorni
Sides & Vegetables

SKIPPING SCHOOL AND GETTING A LESSON IN REAL FOOD

My all-time favourite vegetable is eggplant.

My southern Italian heritage has a beautiful relationship with *melanzane*, which is such a versatile vegetable. We grill it, stuff it, and fry it. Eggplant is also the star ingredient of a beautiful stew called caponata, and enhances a simple pasta dish in *pasta a la norma*. Grilled vegetables would definitely be missing something without the wonderful texture of a perfectly grilled slice of eggplant.

Growing up in southern Ontario, eggplant was always plentiful from late July to early fall, but I didn't always love it. My mother would often stuff it with a blend of ground meats, the pulp from the eggplant, bread and parmesan cheese. As children, we only ate the stuffing and not the outside eggplant shell, thinking we were avoiding this foreign vegetable that none of our friends had even heard of!

As one of the only two Italian families at our local primary school, we grew vegetables that many of my friends were curious about. Sometimes we would leave them drying on cookie sheets in the backyard. I caught my friend tasting some leftover pasta fagioli once as she waited for me to finish the dishes! My family was different than others I knew. I had never had canned soup or macaroni and cheese from a box!

My fondest eggplant memory comes from my days as a high school student in the 1980s. I was in grade 11 and my two cousins, Maria and Louis, were in grade 12. It was a beautiful September day and, being teenagers, we were hungry. Now, most teens would skip school and go to the closest fast food joint, but not us. We went to Nonna's house!

My Nonna Natalizia (who my daughter and I are both named after) lived with Maria's family and lived within walking distance from our school. I still remember strolling up her driveway on a late weekday morning.

Nonna was in the garden and beamed when she saw three of her grandchildren! Nonna was in her sixties when she moved to Canada, and was now in her seventies. She never learned to speak English. She greeted us with a Calabrese greeting that, roughly translated, means "here you are," and she never once asked us why we weren't in school. Of course, her first question was "Are you hungry?"

Nonna went to the garden and picked eggplant, peppers and tomatoes, along with a handful of recently harvested potatoes, and headed to her basement kitchen. Within an hour she presented us with our most favourite Calabrese dish of the harvest season: *Patate, peperoni, melanzane e pomodori* (sliced potatoes with the skin still intact, fried with a medley of eggplant, peppers and tomatoes – recipe on page 83). This, along with a large slice of her homemade bread, was a memorable meal. It just couldn't get any more local or wholesome. And it was served up by a remarkable woman, who wanted nothing more than to grow vegetables, cook and care for her family.

Nonna harvested the garden in the fall of 2002 for the last time. She lived in Canada until she died in March 2003, at the age of 95.

HERB ROASTED BABY POTATOES

Everybody loves these potatoes! Golden brown and flavourful, they often make an appearance on my table with roasted meats. I will boil them and toss them in the herbs ahead and then just roast before serving.

2 lbs. baby potatoes

Virgin olive oil

Salt/pepper

3 tbsp. fresh rosemary

2 tbsp. fresh thyme

2 cloves fresh garlic, minced

Preheat the oven to 450°F. Put the potatoes, with the skin on, in a large pot and cover with water. Bring the pot to a boil. Strain the water and let the potatoes cool slightly.

Take a large sheet pan and cover in parchment paper. Add two tablespoons of olive oil, garlic and herbs. Cut the potatoes in half and add to the pan. Season with salt and pepper. Toss all the ingredients together ensuring the oil is dispersed evenly. Add more as needed.

Bake in the preheated oven until golden brown, 20 minutes or more.

Yield: 4-6 servings

PORTOBELLO MARSALA

This is the vegetarian version of the chicken or veal marsala. I adapted this recipe to satisfy clients who don't eat meat. It has a similar flavour profile with the satisfaction of a meaty portobello! It is easy to make both the meat and vegetarian versions of this dish at the same time, with little effort.

4 large portobello mushroom caps, wiped clean

Salt and pepper

4 tsp. chopped, fresh sage

4 tsp. olive oil

2 tbsp. dry marsala wine

4 tsp. butter, optional

If the gills of the mushrooms are dirty, scoop them out and discard. Place caps on a sheet pan covered in parchment paper, gills up. Season with salt and pepper. Sprinkle the chopped, fresh sage on top. Drizzle with olive oil and dry marsala wine. Place a few pats of butter on top, if using. Bake in a preheated 400°F oven for 20-30 minutes until tender.

Yield: 4 Servings

POTATOES, EGGPLANT, TOMATOES & PEPPERS

My favourite Calabrese dish of the harvest season, this is what Nonna made my cousins and I the day we skipped school and went to her place to eat. Get the full story on page 77!

6-8 plum tomatoes, peeled, seeded and crushed

2 tbsp. olive oil

1 ½ lbs. Italian eggplant, sliced into semi-circles and generously salted, left for 20 minutes, then squeezed to remove liquid

2 tbsp. olive oil, plus more

1 ¼ lbs. peppers, assorted hot and sweet varieties, sliced into strips

2 ½ lbs. of baby white potatoes, sliced with skin on

Vegetable oil

Salt

In a small sauce pan heat 2 tablespoons olive oil and add the crushed tomatoes. Bring to a boil, turn down heat to a simmer until cooked thoroughly and reduced, about 10-15 minutes.

In a large frying pan, heat 2 tablespoons olive oil and sauté eggplant until cooked and slightly golden. Remove to a bowl. Add more olive oil if needed and sauté peppers until cooked. Remove to bowl.

Add about 1 inch of vegetable oil to another frying pan and heat until very hot. Add potatoes and fry until cooked and golden. Remove potatoes with a slotted spoon to the first frying pan. Add the eggplant, peppers and tomato sauce. Mix thoroughly and heat through. Add salt to taste.

Note: Image shows dish before potatoes have been added.

Yield: 4-6 Servings

RAPINI WITH GARLIC & CHILLIES

Rapini or broccoli rabe are one of those vegetables that people either love or hate! I love them. A bitter green loaded with vitamins, they are often found in Southern Italy. In Italy they are often not blanched first and therefore quite bitter. My Mother always blanched them first and I find this tones down the bitterness. I serve them as a side dish or as an unexpected addition to sausage on a bun.

2 tbsp. olive oil

1 bunch rapini, washed and ragged leaves and 1 inch of the course stem removed

Salt

2 cloves garlic, crushed

1 tsp. crushed chillies or more to taste

Bring a large pot of water to boil. Add rapini and boil until the stems are tender.

Drain and let cool.

Heat oil until shimmering in a frying pan. Add garlic and sauté until it is golden. Do not let it brown. Add rapini and coat with oil. Season with salt and the chillies. Sauté until heated through. Taste and adjust the seasoning and chillies to taste.

Yield: 4 Servings

ROASTED ROOT VEGETABLES

This is a great make ahead dish for the holiday table. Get it ready the day before and then just roast before serving. The turmeric adds a beautiful colour to the vegetables without altering the taste. This was a great tip I learned in culinary school!

An assortment of root vegetables such as carrots, turnip, parsnips or rutabaga, cut into sticks

Fresh herbs, such as thyme or rosemary

Salt/pepper

Garlic cloves, minced

Olive oil

1 tsp. ground turmeric, optional

Preheat oven to 450°F. Peel and chop vegetables into sticks about the same size.

Bring a large pot of water to boil. Add the turmeric and vegetables. Blanche for a few minutes until tender crisp. Strain and place in an ice bath to cool.

Once cool, strain water. Place a piece of parchment paper on a sheet pan and add a couple tablespoons of olive oil. Add vegetables, garlic, herbs, salt and pepper. Toss to coat, adding more oil if needed. Bake in oven until heated and caramelized.

Yield: Varies based on size and quantity of raw vegetables

ROASTED SWEET PEPPERS

Roasted peppers are delicious as a side dish or as a condiment for sausage on a bun. Mix the ratio of hot to sweet peppers based on your tolerance for spice. When peppers are in season, I will often roast and freeze them for the winter months.

Assorted sweet and/or hot fresh peppers, washed and air dryed

Good quality extra virgin olive oil

Salt

Heat an outdoor grill on high until very hot. Add the peppers and grill until charred on all sides. They should collapse as they cook.

Cool completely. They can be frozen in bags as this point for future use.

Remove the charred skin, stem, seeds and inside membranes.

Rip the flesh into strips and place in a bowl reserving any juices. Season with salt, taste and adjust seasoning. The pepper flavour should shine.

Add the extra virgin olive oil to taste. I like to add enough to make a sauce for dipping bread.

STUFFED ZUCCHINI

We always get way more zucchini in our garden than we want or need. This is a great side dish or vegetarian entree. Small zucchini are more tender, but if you substitute medium-sized you could slice them to serve.

4 small zucchini, the round variety work well

½ cup fresh breadcrumbs, crusts trimmed, soaked in milk & squeezed dry

6 tbsp. parmesan cheese

2 tbsp. romano cheese, optional

1 egg, beaten

2 tbsp. chopped parsley

2 tbsp. chopped fresh marjoram *OR* 2 tsp. dry

1 garlic clove minced

Pinch nutmeg, grated

Salt & pepper

1 tbsp. olive oil

Boil the zucchini whole until barely tender. Cut the ends off, and slice lengthwise. Make 2 "boats" out of each zucchini by removing the pulp with a spoon.

Preheat the oven to 400°F. Mix everything except the oil in a bowl and stuff the zucchini cavities. Brush with olive oil and bake for 30 minutes until browned.

Yield: 8 Servings

Insalati
Salads

LIQUID GOLD: IS IT REALLY AUTHENTIC?

"Olive oil is one of the most frequently adulterated food products in the EU."

– TOM MUELLER, *EXTRA VIRGINITY: THE SUBLIME AND SCANDALOUS WORLD OF OLIVE OIL*

The best, freshest ingredients make a huge difference to the taste of your meals, and olive oil is no exception. Extra virgin olive oil, *real* extra virgin olive oil, is a foundation of the Mediterranean diet, which is considered one of the healthiest diets in the world.

However, if your olive oil is not authentic extra virgin olive oil, you may not be getting the health benefits from Mediterranean dishes that you're expecting. Only a small percentage of oil on the market that are labelled as "extra virgin" are actually authentic extra virgin olive oil.

Three years ago I made the commitment to only use authentic virgin olive oil and extra virgin olive oil in my kitchen. I only use olive oil from my ancestral hometown in Calabria, and I always cook with authentic virgin olive oil, which has a higher acidic value and higher smoking point. I finish off all my dishes with authentic extra virgin olive oil.

What makes extra virgin olive oil authentic? The most important criterion is that it must be 100% olive oil, and this means *only* olive oil. No colours, no chemicals, no other oils mixed in. This requirement eliminates a number of oils claiming to be extra virgin olive oil right off the bat!

The next requirement is the oil's acidity level. In order to be authentic extra virgin olive oil, your oil must be 0.8% or lower acidity. This eliminates quite a few more olive oil brands, as the majority found in regular grocery stories are blends, low quality olive oil, or adulterated olive oil.

With these requirements in mind, you may be wondering if authentic extra virgin olive oil is worth the extra money and effort. The answer is: **absolutely**. Using authentic extra virgin olive oil as an ingredient alone can elevate your dishes like no other ingredient!

Often, clients tell me, "I prepare your recipes at home but they just don't taste the same." Using an olive oil that is not authentic will always limit the potential of your dishes!

When I travelled to my ancestral hometown in Calabria in October 2015, I visited the local olive grove and olive oil manufacturer for the annual harvest and Olive Oil Festival. I witnessed the production of olive oil, from the harvest to the first oil flowing into the vats. We celebrated with the locals and enjoyed regional specialities prepared with the first oil of the season. The pride and traditions that go into producing the real deal are a marvel to see and experience, and knowing that I use oil produced from the same trees my ancestors used provides me with a sense of joy.

I know where my olive oil comes from, do you?

HOW TO CHOOSE AN AUTHENTIC EXTRA VIRGIN OLIVE OIL

- Buy from a store that allows you to taste it before buying. If possible, buy directly from the producer so that you know exactly know where it is coming from.
- If you notice bitterness or pungency in the taste of the oil, this means antioxidants are present, which is a good thing.
- Check the expiry date or date of harvest! Olive oil is good for up to two years after the harvest date.
- Choose oils stored in a dark glass bottle, which will protect the oil from light.
- Don't worry about the colour of the oil itself. Olive oil can vary in colour, from green to gold.
- Just like we select wines based on grape varieties, look for the listed olive varieties used to make the oil.
- Look for information on the oil's origins. "Product of Italy" is not enough; see if you can find the exact town and region. The family name associated with the oil's production is even better.

BABY GREENS WITH BALSAMIC SOAKED FIGS, GOAT'S CHEESE & PINE NUTS

This is a delicious salad that will impress your friends! The fig seeds give a little texture to the dressing and the figs & balsamic are a natural pairing. You could substitute dried cranberries or any dried fruit for the figs, but figs are my favourite!

½ cup dried figs, stems removed, chopped

3 tbsp. balsamic vinegar from Modena

6 cups baby greens

1 small head of radicchio, shredded

6 tbsp. good quality extra virgin olive oil

Salt & pepper

½ cup fresh goat's cheese, cubed

4 tbsp. toasted pine nuts (optional)

Soak bite size pieces of dried figs in the balsamic vinegar, in a small bowl, at least 15 minutes. Remove just the figs and toss with the baby greens and radicchio in a large bowl. Season with salt and pepper to taste.

Arrange the lettuce and figs on 8 salad plates. Add the cubes of goat's cheese and the pine nuts. Add the extra virgin olive oil to the remaining balsamic in the bowl and whisk until emulsified. Add more olive oil and balsamic at a ratio of 2:1 if needed.

Drizzle on the salad ensuring the goat's cheese is "stained" by the dressing.

Yield: 6-8 Servings

CLASSIC CAPRESE SALAD

Caprese salad is a classic Italian dish. Contrary to popular belief, it is not served with balsamic vinegar. In Italy, as well as in my kitchen, it is served just like this with the finest ingredients available: heirloom tomatoes and basil from my garden, fresh mozzarella (buffalo or cow's milk), and extra virgin olive oil from my ancestral hometown in Calabria. That's it, that's all... That's all you need when they are the finest.

3 garden-fresh seasonal ripe tomatoes

250 grams fresh mozzarella

8-10 tender basil leaves, washed and air-dried

Salt & pepper

Good quality extra virgin olive oil

Wash and slice the tomatoes in ½ inch slices and lay them on the cutting board. Cut the fresh mozzarella into similarly sized slices. (You may need to slice the cheese slices in half if they are too large.) Season tomatoes and cheese with salt and pepper.

On a platter or salad plates, alternate the tomatoes, cheese and basil leaves. Drizzle generously with the best quality extra virgin olive oil. Serve with bread to soak up every drop of olive oil.

Yield: 4-6 Servings

FENNEL & BLOOD ORANGE SALAD

Try this salad in the winter when you're craving something fresh. Both fennel and blood oranges are plentiful in the winter, so they are readily available. The fronds are a beautiful addition and they are an edible garnish!

1 bulb of fennel, washed and dried; sections and fronds removed and saved

1 small red onion

1 cucumber

4 radishes

3 tbsp. good quality white wine vinegar

6 tbsp. good quality extra virgin olive oil

Sea salt

Fresh ground pepper

4 blood oranges, peeled, pith and seeds removed, segmented, juice reserved

Slice the first 4 ingredients very finely with a mandolin. Toss in a bowl with salt and pepper, vinegar and the 6 tablespoons of oil. Add the orange segments and any juice. Taste and adjust seasoning, adding more vinegar and/or oil if necessary.

Arrange on plates and add a few fronds on top. Serve immediately.

Yield: 6-8 Servings

GRILLED VEGETABLE SALAD

This is a great recipe to bring to a BBQ or picnic. When the usual pasta and potato salads make the rounds this will stand out. Served at room temperature, this could be made days ahead and it makes lots. It keeps in the fridge for 4-5 days.

4 long thin/small, round eggplants OR 1 large eggplant

4 zucchini

Salt

1 medium-sized red onion

1 red pepper

1 orange pepper

1 yellow pepper

2 garlic cloves, chopped

2 tbsp. olive oil

For the dressing:

¼ cup good quality extra virgin olive oil

1 garlic clove, crushed

2 tbsp. balsamic vinegar from Modena

3 tbsp. chopped parsley

¼ tsp. sugar

Slice the eggplant and zucchini in thin long strips (a mandolin works great here), and sprinkle with salt. Layer in a colander in the sink for 20 minutes until the bitter water starts to drain. Gently squeeze out excess water. Pat dry with paper towel. Toss in a bowl with 2 tablespoons olive oil and chopped garlic.

Slice the peppers in half and remove the seeds and membranes. Add to the zucchini and eggplant and toss in oil and garlic. Slice the onion in half and trim the root. With the root attaching the segments, slice into semi circles. Brush with olive oil.

Preheat griddle or outdoor grill on high heat. Brush with oil and grill vegetables 1-4 minutes per side until fragrant and with grill marks. Let vegetables cool slightly and chop to an appropriate size. Add to a serving bowl.

Dressing: Add all ingredients in a bowl and whisk thoroughly. Drizzle dressing over room temperature vegetables. Taste and adjust seasoning with salt and pepper.

Yield: 8-10 Servings

SAN GIORGIO TOMATO SALAD

This is my family's tomato salad named after my ancestral hometown in Calabria. Every Italian family has their version; this is ours. It is the simplest of salads and for that reason you really must use the best tomatoes and extra virgin olive oil for this recipe. This is a staple in my house during tomato season and is a cornerstone of the quintessential "antipasto lunch"... a bit of this, a bit of that.

4 of the freshest, in-season, full-size tomatoes you can find (more if they are cocktail or cherry size)

2 cloves of fresh garlic, diced largely

Salt to taste

½ teaspoon good quality Italian oregano

¼ cup of the best quality extra virgin olive oil

Chop the tomatoes into ½ inch cubes. Sprinkle with salt, taste and adjust salt until the tomato flavor shines.

Let this sit for at least 15 minutes so the flavours can blend and the tomatoes emit juices for the sauce.

Add the garlic, which is not intended to eat, but rather flavor the salad. Add the oregano and oil. Stir well and taste. Adjust seasonings and oil as the tomato size will vary.

Serve with crusty bread to soak up the sauce.

Yield: 4 Servings

Dolci
Sweets

VEGETABLES IN CAKE?! NATALINA'S DOUBLE CHOCOLATE ZUCCHINI BREAD

As a mother of four, I am always trying to get my kids to eat healthy. My husband is a successful home gardener, and we are always blessed with the most beautiful bounty of fresh produce from June to September. One of the vegetables we always get way more than we can use is zucchini!

I sauté it with onions and peppers as a great side dish. We stuff it with an herb bread stuffing in one of my Classic Italian I classes. I add it to primavera sauces with pasta, and I make it "a la parmigiana" in place of eggplant. It is a very versatile vegetable.

Unfortunately, my kids would not have any of it when they were young! This is where the sneaky Italian mamma comes in: why not hide it in a dessert? In the late 1990s, we were living in Milan, Italy, and my Italian teacher, Elizabeta, would come to our apartment twice a week for my Italian lessons. We always started out with the Italian course protocol set out by the American company my husband worked for at the time, but inevitably, we always ended up talking about food… in Italian of course! So, although my conversational Italian is very good, my Italian grammar and written Italian leave something to be desired because of this!

Often, I would offer Elizabeta espresso and whatever home baking I had on hand. One day, I offered her some fresh baked zucchini bread with raisins. Well, when I told her what was in it, she was shocked!

"Zucchini, the long green vegetable?!… Impossible! In cake?!"

She tasted it and was pleasantly surprised! She then asked me, quite embarrassedly, if she could bring her Nonna a piece "because she would never believe me if I told her!" Of course I sent a few pieces home with her.

The next time she came her Nonna wanted the recipe!

I make many different zucchini breads but this is my family's favourite! Along with the zucchini, I use heart-healthy olive oil, a mix of white and whole wheat flour, and ground flax. Let them think it's dessert when all these healthy ingredients are in it!

3 eggs

¾ cup olive oil

1 ½ cups sugar

2 tsp. vanilla

3 cups shredded zucchini, with skin left on

1 tsp. cinnamon

1 tsp. salt

2 tsp. baking soda

½ tsp. baking powder

2 ⅓ cups flour (I use 1 cup whole wheat & 1-⅓ all-purpose, plus ⅛ cup ground flax seeds)

¾ cup good quality, unsweetened cocoa

1 cup semi-sweet chocolate chips

½ cup nuts, optional

Preheat the oven to 350°F. Prepare two loaf pans. Wipe with vegetable oil and dust with flour.

With a whisk, beat the eggs, olive oil, sugar and vanilla in a large bowl. Add the grated zucchini, set aside.

In another bowl, thoroughly mix all the dry ingredients and chocolate chips and nuts, if using.

Add the dry ingredients to the wet ensuring it is all mixed well with no dry clumps. Don't overmix.

Divide the batter between the 2 prepared pans and bake for 45-55 minutes, until a knife inserted in the middle comes out clean. Cool completely. Wrap tightly in tin foil for home freezing.

AFFOGATO

Affogato means "drowned". This isn't really dessert, but rather a "special coffee". If we are having a large, multi-course meal, sometimes there just isn't room for dessert, but a sweet finish with coffee is a real treat! Even the kids like this with vanilla ice cream and hot chocolate.

Espresso coffee

4 oz. per person vanilla gelato or ice-cream (1 scoop per person)

Amaretto, ½ oz. per person

Place 1 scoop of gelato or ice-cream in a glass or cup. Pour the Amaretto over top and then pour hot espresso coffee over top. Serve immediately... no sugar or cream required!

Yield : 1 Serving

AMARETTI STUFFED PEACHES

Amaretto and peaches is a classic Italian flavour combination. This is an easy dessert that can come together quickly. It naturally pairs well with Amaretto and although Italians don't usually serve dessert with ice cream it is delicious with good quality vanilla ice cream or gelato!

4 ripe fresh peaches *OR* canned in water or juice, not syrup

⅔ cup crushed amaretti cookies**

2 tbsp. sweet marsala

2 tbsp. butter, softened

½ tsp. vanilla

2 tbsp. sugar

1 egg yolk

Lemon juice, optional

Preheat oven to 350°F. Wash the peaches and remove the stone. Enlarge the stone hole of the peaches with a spoon. Sprinkle with lemon juice if using fresh.

Soak the amaretti crumbs in the Marsala for a few minutes. Add the softened butter along with the remainder of ingredients. Mix well. Fill the stone cavities with the filling and bake for 35-40 minutes.

**If you can't find amaretti cookies substitute large lady fingers, substitute amaretto liqueur for the marsala and add 2 tablespoons ground almonds (optional).

Yield: 6-8 Servings

CLASSIC ZABAGLIONE

This is one of the classics of Italian cooking. It makes a delicious non-dairy cream that is rich and delicious. I like to serve it over berries. Add some to your espresso coffee for a nice treat as well!

4 egg yolks

¼ cup of sugar

½ cup of sweet Marsala

Choose a steel bowl that fits snuggly over a medium-sized pot or use a double boiler. Add a small amount of water to the pot .

Beat the egg yolks and sugar in the bowl until pale and fluffy. Continue to beat while adding the marsala a little at a time. Place the pot or double boiler on the heat. Place the bowl over barely simmering water over low heat, stirring continuously, until the mixture starts to rise. This will take a while. The mixture will get thicker and form soft peaks.

Remove from the heat and serve hot or cold on it's own, or over fruit.

Yield: 4 Servings

COFFEE GRANITA

Granita is served all over Italy, but especially in Sicily. It is a refreshing, light treat and this can replace an after dinner espresso when the weather is warm. With no special equipment required to make it, granita is super easy!

2 cups water

½ cup granulated sugar

1 cup very strong espresso coffee, cooled

Boil the water and sugar together and remove from heat and cool. Combine the cooled water and cooled coffee together in a shallow steel pan. Place in the freezer and scrape with a fork every hour until a slushy consistency is achieved. Serve as an after dinner "frozen coffee" or light dessert.

Yield : 6-8 Servings

LEMON GRANITA

Try this recipe with different varieties of lemons such as Meyer, or mix different citrus fruit and only add sugar to taste. It makes a nice light dessert or palate cleanser between courses.

2 cups water

½ cup granulated sugar

Grated zest of 1 lemon, scrubbed before grating

Juice of 2 large lemons

Heat the water and sugar until the sugar dissolves, bring to a boil. Remove from the heat and allow to cool.

Add the lemon juice and zest. Place in a shallow stainless steel container and freeze. Place in the freezer and scrape with a fork every hour until a slushy consistency is achieved. .

Yield : 6 Servings

NONNA'S LEMON COOKIES (UNCLE PAUL'S ADAPTATION)

These are the cookies that I grew up with and my children grew up with! These are "dunking cookies". Dunk them in coffee, milk, tea or whatever is your pleasure. Nonna always has them on hand for when the grandchildren stop by. They are so synonymous with Nonna that when we lived in Italy I made them one afternoon. When I met my kids at the bus stop after school I announced I had a surprise and produced the cookies. My oldest exclaimed "Nonna is here!"

6 large eggs

1 ½ cups of granulated sugar

Zest of 4 lemons

1 ¾ cups vegetable oil

1 tbsp. vanilla

1 cup of whole milk, heated

6 ½ tsp. of baking powder

7 cups of flour

Vegetable shortening to grease the pans

In the large bowl of a stand mixer with the whisk attachment, beat the eggs and the sugar on high speed, until fluffy, about 15 minutes. Adjust speed to low and add the lemon zest, vegetable oil, vanilla and heated milk. Remove the whisk attachment and switch to the dough hook.

In a seperate bowl, mix the flour and baking powder with a whisk.

Start adding the dry mixture to the wet, 2 cups at a time. Continue adding the dry ingredients and alternatively mixing. You may have to remove the bowl and continue mixing by hand. You could also put the dough on the counter and knead the dough to fully incorporate all the flour until you have an elastic dough.

Preheat the oven to 350°F.

Grease cookie sheets lightly with vegetable shortening.

Take a piece of dough and roll it into a snake about ½ inch in diameter and 6 inches long. Place it in a "U" shape and alternating with each side, overlap the other side until you get a braided like shape. This is my Mom's classic shape for these cookies. You could also just roll out a snake 1 inch in diameter and cut sticks about 4 inches long.

Bake these in a preheated oven until fully cooked and golden brown. Depending on the size, it could be 20 minutes or more.

Yield: Lots!

PANNA COTTA WITH BLUEBERRY COMPOTE

Panna cotta is a simple, easy dessert that everyone loves. "Panna" means cream and "cotta" means cooked. It's not quite custard, but a cross between a pudding and a jello. Experiment with different seasonal fruits. I love to mix strawberries and rhubarb from the garden, or peaches when they are in season.

1 cup 35% cream	*Topping:*
3 cups milk	2 cup blueberries
½ cup sugar	¼ cup sugar
2 tsp. vanilla	1 tsp. corn starch
2 packs unflavoured gelatin *or* 5 tsp. loose	(You may substitute seasonal fruit for the blueberries, sweeten as needed)

Heat cream and 2 ¾ cups of milk in a saucepan over medium heat. Stir in sugar, vanilla. Continue until it is simmering.

Meanwhile, sprinkle gelatin over remaining milk in a medium bowl for 2-3 minutes. Pour the warm milk over the gelatin and stir with a whisk. Let the gelatin dissolve. Divide among 6 cups and refrigerate until set, 2 hours to overnight. If you want to remove from cups, loosen first with a sharp knife and turn over on a plate.

Heat berries with sugar and cornstarch and cool. Top Panna Cotta.

Yield : 6-8 Servings

TORTA DI MELE - APPLE CAKE

Apple cake is to Italy like apple pie is to North America. It is a staple dessert. Often yogurt is used as it ensures a moist cake. The addition of olive oil also ensures a richness and it is much healthier than butter. The apple and almond flavour combination is one that is used often, and the crunchy topping adds a coffee cake like texture. I often use whatever apples I have on hand – usually the wrinkled ones in the back of the crisper that come back in the lunch bags!

1 ½ cups all purpose flour

¾ cups granulated sugar

1 ½ tsp. baking powder

½ tsp. baking soda

¼ tsp. salt

2 eggs

⅔ cup plain Greek yogurt

¼ cup olive oil

½ tsp. almond extract

½ tsp. cinnamon

3 apples, peeled and thinly sliced

Topping:

3 Tbsp. sliced almonds

½ tsp. granulated sugar

½ tsp. cinnamon

In bowl, stir together flour, sugar, baking powder, baking soda, and salt.

In separate bowl, beat eggs, stir in yogurt, olive oil and almond extract. Stir wet ingredients into flour mixture until just combined. Pour into greased 9-inch springform pan. Arrange apples over batter.

Topping: Combine almonds, sugar, and cinnamon and sprinkle over apples in pan.

Bake in 350°F oven for 50 minutes to 1 hour until cake tester comes out clean.

Cool before removing from springform pan and serving.

Yield : 8 Servings

VENETIAN RICE PUDDING
WITH MARSALA-SOAKED FIGS

Now this is not like any rice pudding you grew up with! The addition of the Marsala-soaked figs elevates this dish and the Arborio rice gives it a very creamy texture. Think of this as a sweet version of risotto... so what's not to like?

2 ½ cups of whole milk

1 cup 35% cream

1 tsp. vanilla extract

¼ cup sugar

¼ tsp. cinnamon

Pinch nutmeg

1 tbsp. grated orange zest

⅔ cup dried figs, chopped

2 tbsp. sweet Marsala

½ cup Arborio rice

Put the milk and cream in a heavy bottomed saucepan and just bring to a boil, then remove from the heat.

Add the sugar, cinnamon, nutmeg and orange zest to milk and cream mixture, and set aside.

Put the figs in a bowl with the Marsala to soak and set aside.

Add the rice to the infused milk and return to the heat.

Bring to a simmer and stir slowly for about 35 minutes or until the rice is almost cooked.

Stir in the figs and the soaking Marsala.

Remove from the heat. Let it cool down and the rice will continue to cook.

Serve at room temperature or warm. It is nice with a scoop of vanilla ice cream.

Yield : 6 Servings

NONNA'S BLUE BOWL

I started baking at the age of 11. I read cookbooks from the library, like a novel, cover to cover. I didn't start to cook savoury dishes until much later.

My mother is a fabulous cook, so most of our conversations took place in the kitchen. Unlike me, my mother is a very precise cook. She would perfect a cookie recipe right down to the pan and brand of ingredients. Once she perfected it, it was always recreated exactly the same way.

It was hard for her to teach us many of her recipes because part of it was written down and part of it was created by memory. By the time I was a teenager, we settled into a regular weekend routine. My mom would make a beautiful, authentic, Italian Sunday *Pranzo* (formal Italian lunch) and I would make some elaborate dessert from the latest cookbook I was reading. My four brothers were the perfect taste testers. I quickly gained confidence.

At age 21, I got married. A couple of months before the wedding my mother told me I needed to learn to cook, so I would help her prepare Sunday lunch from now on. A few weeks in she quickly recognized that I had been paying attention and I could, in fact, cook as well as bake! Much to my brothers' delight, we went back to our usual routine.

Once I got married and moved away from home, I finally had my own kitchen. I remember planning our first meal as husband and wife the day after we got home from our honeymoon: roast chicken, potatoes, and vegetables. While driving home from work at 6 p.m., I quickly realized that – if we wanted to eat anytime soon, I was going to have to pick up a rotisserie chicken in place of my homecooked chicken.

I soon realized that my mom was the quickest, easiest source of information for meal planning and execution. I would regularly call her with questions about meal planning, family recipes, which ingredients to buy, and more. After the meal, she always got a follow-up phone call discussing what worked and what didn't. The reply, often, from my perfectionist mother was: "Next time, do it this way...".

On one particular occasion, I decided I was going to make fresh pasta for the first time on my own. My aunts had gifted me a manual pasta machine as a housewarming gift when we bought our first house, and I still use it to this day in my school! So I made the call: "Mom, what is your fresh pasta recipe?"

Her reply:"Well, you know that blue bowl? I fill it up with flour, not full like a mountain, but more like a hill."

And so began "Weekends with Mamma". Me with my scale, measuring cups and measuring spoons, and my mom with her wonderful family recipes and food memories.

This, my friends, is when I decided that I needed to start recording these recipes, if only just for family. I would have never guessed all those years ago that some of those recipes would be precious additions to my first cookbook.

Menus

6 CLASSIC ITALIAN FOUR-COURSE MENUS

Page Numbers for Recipes Noted in Brackets

Menu #1
Seasonal Salad: San Giorgio Tomato Salad (103) or Fennel Salad (99)
Seasonal Risotto: Mushroom (39), Asparagus (41) or Squash (43)
Veal or Chicken Marsala with Sage & Mushrooms (75)
Amaretti Stuffed Peaches (109)

Menu #2
Classic Caprese Salad (97)
Ricotta & Spinach Stuffed Pasta Shells (33)
Baked Salmon with Fennel (63)
Venetian Rice Pudding with Marsala Soaked Figs (123)

Menu #3
Grilled Vegetable Salad (101)
Rigatoni with Meatballs and Sausage (47)
Stuffed Zucchini (91)
Panna Cotta with Blueberry Compote (119)

Menu #4
Basil Pesto & Goat's Cheese Crostini (13)
Milanese Minestrone with Rice (53)
Pan Pizza with Basil Pesto and Cheese (25)
Granita: Coffee (113) or Lemon (115)

Menu #5
Baby Greens with Balsamic Soaked Figs, Goat's Cheese and Pine Nuts (95)
Classic Potato Gnocchi (35)
Italian Braised Beef in Wine with Wild Mushrooms (69) & Roasted Root Vegetables (87)
Classic Zabaglione (111) with Seasonal Fruit

Menu #6
Bruschetta (15)
Fresh Egg Pasta (31) with Tomato Basil Sauce (51)
Chicken Parmigiana (65)
Rapini with Garlic and Chillies (85)
Affogato (107)

NATALINA'S KITCHEN · BRINGING HOMEMADE BACK ·

TABLE OF EQUIVALENTS

The exact equivalents in the following tables have been rounded for convenience.

US/UK

oz = ounce
lb = pound
tsp = teaspoon
tbsp = tablespoon
fl. oz. = fluid ounce
qt = quart

Metric

g = gram
kg = kilogram
mm = millimetre
cm = centimetre
ml = millilitre
l = litre

Weights

US/UK	METRIC
1 oz	30 g
2 oz	60 g
3 oz	30 g
4 oz (¼ lb)	125 g
5 oz (1/3 lb)	155 g
6 oz	185 g
7 oz	220 g
8 oz (½ lb)	250 g
10 oz	315 g
12 oz (¾ lb)	375 g
14 oz	440 g
16 oz (1 lb)	500 g
1½ lb	750 g
2 lb	1 kg
3 lb	1.5 kg

Lengths

US/UK	METRIC
1/8 in	3 mm
1/4 in	6 mm
1/2 in	12 mm
1 in	2½ cm
2 in	5 cm
3 in	7½ cm
4 in	10 cm
5 in	13 cm
6 in	15 cm
7 in	18 cm
8 in	20 cm
9 in	23 cm
10 in	25 cm
11 in	28 cm
12 in / 1 ft	30 cm

Liquids

US	METRIC	UK
2 tbsp	30 ml	1 fl oz
1/4 cup	60 ml	2 fl oz
1/3 cup	80 ml	3 fl oz
1/2 cup	125 ml	4 fl oz
2/3 cup	160 ml	5 fl oz
3/4 cup	180 ml	6 fl oz
1 cup	250 ml	8 fl oz
1½ cups	375 ml	12 fl oz
2 cups	500 ml	16 fl oz
4 cups / 1 qt	1 L	32 fl oz

Oven Temperatures

FAHRENHEIT	CELSIUS	GAS
250	120	½
275	140	1
300	150	2
325	160	3
350	180	4
375	190	5
400	200	6
425	220	7
450	230	8
475	240	9
500	260	10

NATALINA'S KITCHEN · BRINGING HOMEMADE BACK ·

CREDITS

A project of this magnitude would not have been possible without the help and support of many people and organizations. Special thanks to Innovation Guelph, Heather Watterworth, Anna Wells, and my family for their support.

Food & Garden Photography
Natalina Bombino Campagnolo
Page 80 and 120: Adobe Stock
Page 132: All photos by Natalina Bombino Campagnolo

Portrait and Kitchen Photography
Trina Koster Photography

Marketing & Branding
Anna Wells

Graphic Design
Snow Conrad

Creative Direction
Heather Watterworth

ABOUT THE AUTHOR

Natalina Bombino Campanolo inspires, educates and delights home cooks and foodies with the vibrant food culture of her Southern Italian heritage.

A trusted and credible source of Italian cooking tips, techniques and authentic Italian recipes, Natalina has helped thousands of people bring homemade food back to their tables, through hands-on cooking classes, videos, and domestic and international food and wine tours.

A wife and mother of four, Natalina spends the majority of her time in the kitchen developing recipes and cooking for her family. She embraces and encourages the elements of the "Italian Mamma" lifestyle – family, food, passion and love – successfully blending it with the 21st century approach of a hip, multi-tasking, social media-savvy female entrepreneur.

Follow Natalina's culinary adventures on social media.

f *natalinaskitchen*   🐦 *@natalinaskitch*   📷 *@natalinaskitchen*

ABOUT NATALINA'S KITCHEN

Italian Cooking Classes

Since September 2011, Natalina has offered hands-on cooking classes from her professional teaching kitchen in Guelph, Ontario, Canada. After six years, her more than 20 different Italian cooking classes are consistently sold out, with additional students turning to waiting lists and private group classes to get a taste of Natalina's passion for Italian food culture.

Beginning in 2017, Natalina will share her most popular classes, recipes, tips and techniques via webcast, so Italian food lovers around the world can bring homemade food back to their tables with help from the Italian Mamma they always wished they had.

For more information on classes and tours, visit italiancookingschoolguelph.com.

Food & Wine Tours

Each year, Natalina leads both domestic and international tours to explore the local food and wine cultures of overlooked destinations in Canada, Italy and the Mediterranean.

Past international tours have visited Italy's Puglia region, Sicily and Malta.

No matter the destination, these small group tours travel off the beaten path to provide a rare immersion in local food and wine culture – including private touring, remarkable accommodations, and unforgettable hands-on culinary experiences.

RECIPE INDEX

NATALINA'S KITCHEN · BRINGING HOMEMADE BACK ·